Rani Dubé was born in India. She remembers rising early to walk in the woods hoping to catch a glimpse of Gandhi on his early morning walk; at age five leading a procession of the freedom movement shouting 'English quit India'; the magic summer nights; the valleys of kingfishers and wild flowers; and one morning in 1947 looking out of the window on a scene of desolation – bodies in the road, houses on fire and a line of refugees already on the move.

She has lived in England for twenty years and began her broadcasting career with the B.B.C. World Service. She has been a producer for the Hindi Service, a successful interviewer and a translator. She was also an editor for Theatre 625. She left the B.B.C. to become a freelancer and learn about film making, and two years ago formed a film company, Parakeet Productions Limited.

Rani Dubé lives in Kent with her husband and their five children.

THE EVIL WITHIN
RANI DUBÉ

Ω————————————————————————

Edited by Timeri Murari

QUARTET BOOKS
LONDON MELBOURNE NEW YORK

Published by Quartet Books Limited 1978
A member of the Namara Group
27 Goodge Street, London W1P 1FD

Copyright © 1978 by Rani Dubé

ISBN 0 7043 2161 0

Printed in Great Britain by litho at The Anchor Press Ltd
and bound by Wm Brendon & Son Ltd
both of Tiptree, Essex

Typeset by Clerkenwell Graphics

THE EVIL WITHIN

For Naim without whom
this book would not
have been possible

CONTENTS

1 The journey

The impersonal voice of the air hostess came over the tannoy: 'Ladies and gentlemen, we will soon be landing in Delhi. The weather is fair, so we hope the landing will be smooth. If you look out of the window you will see the vast expanse of the Indo-Gangetic plain.'

I looked and saw the soft browns, the beiges and gold and an occasional green stretching as far as the horizon. Excitement fluttered inside me like the wings of a bird as I wondered how India would seem now after the ending of the nineteen-month Emergency and the startling defeat of Mrs Gandhi in the elections. It was strange that, however many times a year I came to India, this same feeling of excitement always moved me. I suppose it is because my sense of belonging to this country goes far deeper than the wounds caused by twenty years of exile.

How well I remember the first time I left India. I was just nineteen and felt that life stretched before me like the vast Ganges plain itself. India, too, was then newly independent and full of almost adolescent hopes and dreams. Nehru was the Prime Minister, and he had a very definite place among the world's statesmen. Nehru, who personified India, had introduced the ancient concepts of 'Panchsheel' into the world of diplomacy in 1953. He had passionately elaborated on respect for sovereignty and friendship, and love for all nations. The then nascent Third

7

World had suddenly discovered a Messiah who made it possible for them to bargain for a place in the sun without being either pro-Russian or pro-American. They could all be non-aligned nations and take help from anyone who offered it. India still had her problems: people were doubtful about Nehru's decisions to emphasize heavy industrialization and to linguistically divide India. But then we were young, and the problems did not look insurmountable. There was still enthusiasm and hope among the people. Nehru always succeeded in making everyone feel that this was our country, our problems, and that we were all working towards solving them together. There was never a 'them' *versus* 'us' feeling. It seemed a far cry indeed from what the newspapers had been saying about Mrs Gandhi's régime.

I still remember Nehru with considerable warmth, but maybe I am a little biased about him. I knew him over a long time. My family had contact with him over a number of years.

Way back in the days of the British Empire, during the Freedom Movement, when my father was still a young man and much involved in the movement, Nehru had visited Meerut, my father's home town. He had listened to some of my father's speeches. This was the time when Mr Pyare Lal Sharma was one of the leading lights of the Freedom Movement in Uttar Pradesh. Mr Sharma had openly declared my father to be his heir apparent in the leadership of the movement. Nehru was much impressed by what he saw in my father – impressed enough to ask my grandmother if she would like to send my father to Allahabad where the Nehru family could take care of his education. My grandmother was very touched, but she politely declined. Widowed and poor she may have been, but she was proud, so she decided that she was going to educate her son herself, and that was that. Nehru, however, kept in touch from then on.

When India became free, my father insisted that he didn't want to remain in politics. He decided that his job was done. He hadn't taken part in the movement for any personal rewards. India was free, and that was all he had ever wanted. Now he just wanted to write, but this decision didn't sever the link between him and Nehru. The world of politics and that of a writer are far apart, but in this case a bridge was provided by the famous Hindi poet Bal Krishna Sharma 'Navin', who was also a much revered politician and a member of parliament. He was my father's best friend and a close friend of Nehru. So the link had remained. Later, when I was older and just beginning to participate in acting and debates, I met Nehru in my own right. I remember how shortly before I left for England we met in the University of Delhi. He had come to preside over some function which I too was attending. He asked what I wanted to do now, and I told him all about my plans to go to England. He gave me a long lecture about not making my stay abroad too long because India needed young people like me. It was an odd relationship, if one can call it that – we kept meeting at functions where I either sang something or won an award for some competition, and he presided over the ceremony and gave the award. It happened so many times that it became a joke between us. Years later, we met in London once, and he recalled how I had sung the National Anthem solo on his first birthday celebrations in free India. I was very moved, but that I suppose was a part of the charisma of Nehru – his involvement with his people. I remember so many anecdotes that Mr 'Navin' would tell after a session in Parliament to illustrate the generosity of Nehru. One concerned the time when a member of the opposition gave Nehru a rough ride in his speech. But it was a good speech, and when the session ended Nehru pointedly went over to the man, put an arm around his shoulders and said, 'That was brilliant. But you did forget a couple of points. Now if I were you, next time I would remember these as well . . .' and went on to elaborate the weak points of his own policy. The man was enchanted, and so was everybody else within earshot. Nehru had charm and political maturity, and he was an intellectual. Sometimes these very qualities became a drawback. He had such an understanding of the other side of an argument that it could be difficult for him to make decisions. I used to say that Nehru should have been our Prime Minister fifty years later, and then maybe we would have been mature enough to cope with his kind of understanding.

In 1947 there was a fierce pride in me about India, Nehru and our newly acquired freedom. I recall that just before I got into the plane which was to bring me to England, I picked up a fistful of the earth of India, put it on my forehead and shut my eyes to wish that I would not be parted from this earth of my country for too long. When I opened my eyes, I found myself looking straight into the eyes of a bewildered American. He had witnessed the whole thing and couldn't understand it. So I tried to explain that it was a way of making a wish and receiving the blessing of my country. He still looked bewildered as he climbed the steps of the aeroplane. At the top of the steps he shook his head and wiped his face with the back of his hand as if to say, 'I would never understand Indians, however long I lived here.'

How different India has become today. Over the years, despair seemed to have overpowered hope. India hadn't taken great progressive strides, but rather had stumbled along, coping with the problem of survival. The problems of unemployment, poverty and overpopulation had remained the same as ever. What had increased was corruption and decay, as though some new kind of cancer had set in and was slowly eating away the soul of India. During my various trips back to India in the last twenty years, I had broken my heart over it again and again. It seemed to me that we were fast losing what was good in our culture, and replacing it with nothing except a general chaos. Everything seemed to be slowly coming to a halt. Offices had become so inefficient that they hardly functioned at all. Students had developed into an enormous problem, with their frustration at the lack of jobs awaiting them after they qualified. It seemed that the situation could never improve. So time and again the students took the law into their own hands. Then politicians used this discontent for their own advantage, and student agitation became frequent and violent about anything and everything. The situation had got so out of hand that teachers were afraid of their students and examinations had become a mere formality – no one dared to fail anyone for fear of violent reprisals.

Meanwhile fanatical religious organizations were flourishing. There were too many strikes in industry, and it looked as though India was being used and prepared for a Marxist takeover.

It hurt so much whenever I thought about the years my father and thousands like him had spent in jail. This India was certainly not what they had fought for. Then Mrs Gandhi emerged as the leader of the country. People were delighted. 'India needs a strong leader,' everyone said. And, for a while, it looked as though she could do no wrong. The Bangladesh crisis made her one of the most popular leaders India had ever had. The world was behind her, and people said openly that she was greater than her father. She had handled the Congress Party brilliantly by cutting the dead wood out of it and splitting it in two in 1969. Everyone had felt that now India wouldn't look back. But alas, fate had a few ideas of its own.

I was shaken out of my world of thoughts and memories by the air hostess asking me to fasten my safety belt. The plane was beginning to circle Delhi now. I could see the morning mist above the trees and the minarets. Delhi slept in the mist, and the breeze swayed the mist slowly around the domes, the towers and the pools. She looked like some forgotten city under water. It was as though she had no life of her own, as though she would sleep in the depths of the ocean unless some Prince Charming or a holy man arrived, and either gave the kiss of life or chanted the magic word for the waves to part and a throbbing, alive and vibrant city to emerge.

The landing was smooth, and the customs were not too difficult. One of them did ask what I had come to do. I thought quickly, and said, 'I want to write a book about India. After all, you have just had a bloodless revolution, haven't you?'

'I suppose you can describe it as that, but I really think it was just that the people had had enough of the corruption and the cruelties and this was their chance to get even,' the customs officer answered.

'Oh, come now, those things are not new to Indians, there has always been corruption here,' I said, thinking he was over-simplifying the whole thing.

'Not to this extent, never. But I had better leave it to you to find out. One thing is certain, you must be careful because one side will be willing to talk a lot and the other will want to say nothing. Have you brought any gadgets, transistors, television, watches, etcetera?' He looked at me.

'No, I brought those years ago. Now it's simple little things, not dutiable,' I said.

He grinned and said, 'OK, have a nice stay.'

I thanked him and walked on. I had chosen not to tell the customs officer the real purpose of my present visit to India. I had really come to write a book about Mrs Gandhi. I had written to her from London and explained what I wanted to do. I had also found a friend of hers who was willing to recommend the idea to Mrs Gandhi, and this would ensure my meeting her.

I had known Nehru, but not his daughter, Mrs Gandhi. In

fact I could remember meeting her only once before. When the election results which dislodged her from power became public, the world press had reacted very strongly. Criticisms of her régime had poured in. People seemed to have forgotten how much they had raved about her achievements earlier. Just because she had lost the election didn't mean that she had failed to achieve a lot during her eleven years in power. I wondered, as I read the papers, if any of them remembered their own leading articles during the Bangladesh crisis. How the world had rallied round her in that moment!

In a strange way, throughout the Emergency, when the world press was screaming about her being a dictator, my sympathies had been with her. I knew how the Indian press needed no gagging. Their love for their privileges was the only gag they ever required. I also knew how that many times in my life India had made me feel extremely authoritarian. I too had wished that I had absolute power to stop the corruption, blackmarketeering, unemployment. I also knew that in 1966, when Mrs Gandhi began her career as the leader of our country, she was known as a woman of steel who was full of ideals and whose personal integrity was without question.

Despite the press reports, I had been unable to believe that anything could have changed a person as drastically as all that. I had also seen the immediate effects of the Emergency. Most of them had been good. The bureaucracy had begun to function, the student agitations had stopped, the crippling strikes had disappeared, prices had come down and, at least on the surface, hoarding and blackmarketeering both had become relatively rare. No mean achievement for any Prime Minister.

So I felt that what Mrs Gandhi needed at this moment was a book written about her as a person. A book about Mrs Gandhi, the human being. Her hopes, her fears, her loves and so on. I thought that if she allowed me to record a series of interviews or conversations, then on the basis of those I could do precisely that. I was also convinced that if the world knew more about her as a person, then it would become that much more easy to assess her political achievements or failures. Now I needed to persuade her to trust me, and I did know that that might prove difficult because her experience with the Indian press hadn't been a particularly pleasant one.

Still, I was willing to have a go. I came out through the customs to meet my parents. I touched their feet and got their blessing. In the taxi, I told my father briefly about the purpose of my visit. He was very excited, and the journalist in him at once responded to the challenge and the possibilities. But he had been a writer and a journalist too long not to know how impossible the task ahead of me was. He tried to warn me, and said, 'I don't think it will be possible for her to talk to you. It will land her and her son Sanjay in deeper waters.'

I laughed in my innocence and thought my father must be exaggerating. At least I hoped he was.

It wasn't as it happened difficult to persuade Mrs Gandhi's secretary to allow me to go and see her. I was told that I could come to No. 1 Safdar Jung Road at 1.30 p.m. that day. No promises were held out, as it was such short notice. If the lunch was not too long, she would spare me a few minutes.

As I travelled in the taxi towards No. 1 Safdar Jung Road, I wondered what she would be like now: Nehru's daughter; India's Prime Minister for eleven years; certainly the world's most powerful woman politician in the last fifty years. She had come into her own really only after her father's death. He had kept her very much in the background. She had acted as his hostess, but that was all. There was speculation about why Nehru hadn't allowed her to come into the limelight more, but nobody was quite sure of the reason. During Nehru's lifetime, people had known her as a stunningly beautiful woman who was also intelligent and accomplished. Nehru had always adored her. He had also suffered from considerable guilt for never having spent enough time with his only child. His commitments with, first of all, the Indian Freedom Movement, and later with the Government of India, had been too many. He had tried to compensate his daughter by writing to her very regularly from wherever he was, but people always doubted whether he or she had felt that the compensation was adequate.

On the whole, she had a lonely childhood. The image of a little girl in that large, palatial, ancestral home of the Nehrus has often haunted me. She must have been a lonely child because all she had for company was her old grandmother and the servants.

Occasionally her aunts would drop in for a flying visit, but that still left most of her days empty. Her much-adored mother died when she was still a very young girl. Her loneliness was such a contrast to the other side of her very privileged childhood, for she also met great personalities, lived in affluence, was educated abroad. This is what the world knows of her, and it is a very real side of her. And in fact it helped her greatly during the days when her popularity was at its peak, because she already had the poise and the ability to move with ease among the most privileged of the land. But the lonely little girl left her mark on Mrs Gandhi's personality. It made her aloof, a little mistrustful and a little cold.

She came into power after Mr Lal Bahadur Shastri's death. India was then feeling the loss of Nehru still. Mr Shastri was loved, but the Indians needed the Nehru charisma. We have always needed to worship our leaders, so the time was right for Mrs Gandhi. She had already begun to shape up as a politician of considerable stature. She had already been President of the Congress Party of India, and a very successful Minister of Information and Broadcasting. At the outset, she took over the premiership as a stop-gap. Nobody thought she would be able to consolidate herself and the Congress Party enough to last. But everybody had underestimated her ability and her strength. She brought about what amounted to a mini-revolution in the Congress Party in 1969. The older and more conservative party men such as the present Prime Minister, Morarji Desai, were weeded out ruthlessly. However, they clung to the Congress name tag, appropriately calling themselves 'Congress Old'. Mrs Gandhi's Congress was known as Congress R (ruling). She manoeuvred herself so brilliantly that not even the seasoned politicians could quite see what hit them. The people of India felt that at last they had a leader of towering strength. The 1971 elections proved their love for her, and she came in with a sweeping majority. This is when things began to go wrong, which eventually led to the Emergency. First came the crisis of Bangladesh. She had the world and India absolutely behind her, but the crisis crippled India economically. Immediately after that came three successive droughts, and the people began to be disillusioned. And there was a period in the early 1970s when political unrest and strikes and the food situation brought Indian democracy almost to a standstill.

Mrs Gandhi was still a very popular leader, but people were beginning to question many things. An inquiry was being demanded into the affairs of her son Sanjay Gandhi's small car factory, Maruti Limited. Gujarat had had its state government threatened by students, and in fact the state administration in Gujarat was so unpopular because of rampant corruption and the high rate of unemployment that a fully-fledged students' movement began which only came to a halt after the State Government was forced to resign. Mrs Gandhi herself had a court case going forward against her. It had been brought by her persistent political rival, Mr Raj Narayan, for alleged malpractices during the 1971 elections. In fact, it looked as though a storm was gathering against Mrs Gandhi.

From the dizzy heights where she was adored by her people, she had descended to a level where she had to answer questions about her electioneering tactics. The results of the Gujarat elections, in which the Congress Party lost heavily, coincided with the High Court judgement against Mrs Gandhi. The Gujarat students had proved that they were no longer willing to support a corrupt régime, even if it was headed by the Congress Party. And as if this was not shock enough in itself – for after all, the Congress Party had been the unquestioned ruling party of India for thirty years – to add to it, not only had a court case been possible against Nehru's daughter, but a judgement was passed finding her guilty.

Add to all this the rest of the chaos of strikes, agitations in other states and Mrs Gandhi's own rocky position with her party. Because all those people that she had taken power from were now ready to get their own back. Despite the High Court judgement against her, she couldn't hand over the power and be certain that after she had coped with the High Court they would allow her to come back into the office of Prime Minister. After all, she herself had only come in as a stop-gap and had simply remained. She had little choice if she wanted to hang on to her chair – the Emergency was the only answer.

There is one more factor that we have to take into consideration, and this is Mrs Gandhi's own personality. As we have said, she is a very beautiful woman, but is also extremely intelligent and articulate. However, she has always had one great failing: she has always been prone to flattery. This has made her unable to select her circle of friends rationally. For some reason, she has always surrounded herself not with those who were truly loyal to her, but with those who are known for their glib tongues and loyalty only to themselves.

Promilla Kalhan, in her book *Black Wednesday*, quotes two letters from Mr Bhawani Prasad Bannerji, the former member of All-India Congress Committee and its Permanent Secretary from 1963 to 1965. The first letter, dated 18 September 1972, contained a warning about 'a new fascist tendency' that was 'steadily growing up in the States'.

> Those who are in power either in the Government or in the Organization are making determined efforts to liquidate all opposition even within the party. Even physical liquidation is becoming part of the game. This is so about the Youth Congress and Chatra Parishad in some places. Very often we criticize the administration and talk of corrupt and uncommitted bureaucracy as the main stumbling block to our progress towards socialism. Even if this is conceded is it ever possible to reform the administration without bringing minimum honesty, character and ideological clarity and conviction at a political level? This purging and restoration of character, laying down a code of public conduct, must begin with the ruling party.

In another letter, dated 13 January 1975, Mr Bannerji informed Mrs Gandhi that:

> Things are moving quite fast in the political arena of the country. You have raised the stature of India in the international sphere far beyond anybody's imagination. But within the country disruptive forces seem to be determined today to somehow foil your plan and weaken you so that they may get you within their grip. This is not only the effort of the Opposition Party or J.P. [Narayan]'s Movement but there are also hidden efforts within the Party in that direction.

> Myself and some others we strongly feel that weakening you at this critical juncture will not only create a danger for democracy but shall also shake the stability of our Nation.

He went on to say:

> I feel deeply anguished and perturbed because I do not have

much faith in the loyalty and bona fides or even in the capacity and capability of many of those whom I see around you. You should have some persons in the organization as well as in the Government who would be loyal to you above everything else. I would urge you to act immediately on this before the cobweb is woven and tightens around you.

Mr Bannerji's letters were not the only ones she received. There were hundreds of letters in which people tried to warn her that the caucus around her wished to put Sanjay in power so that they could themselves move in and continue to rob the people of India. It was even hinted that her own life could be in danger, since these people would brush aside anybody who got in the way of their ambitions. But Mrs Gandhi took no notice, and it was already too late. The sycophants in the caucus surrounding her had already tightened the cobwebs so she could not hear or see, and she only spoke that which was expected of her by the caucus. Her love of flattery, her inability to be more selective in the choice of her friends, was also a big cause of the declaration of the Emergency on 25 June 1975.

The architects of the Emergency were the members of the caucus around her. The Emergency gagged the press and took away from the people of India the rights of appeal against arrest. People could be arrested for any length of time without trial. The police were given extra powers which made them the supreme authorities in the land. The whole country developed overnight a sense of fear because of the many plain-clothes men watching and prying into people's lives. An air of 'Big Brother is watching you' prevailed everywhere. People talked in whispers. Samachar, a news agency, was specially created by the Government to give out the only sort of news which the newspapers were allowed to print. Samachar's job was not only to provide news approved by the caucus, but also to circulate fictitious news about Mrs Gandhi's and the caucus's rivals. In other words, the real news was suppressed and rumour-mongering was encouraged.

This, on the whole, had an insidious effect, because it provided protection for the excesses of the vasectomy drives, the arbitrary demolition of shanty-towns or any other kind of atrocity committed by the caucus. People were not entirely deprived of news, essentially because India has a long tradition of passing information by word of mouth. But still the known news remained only a fraction of what was really happening in India. On the whole, the people were told only of the positive side of the Emergency – they were informed when a blackmarketeer was put in jail, they were told how prices had come down and how food hoarding had stopped. They were not told how many thousand ordinary social workers had been jailed without trial, or how much corruption was prevalent in higher circles.

The fear also aided Sanjay and his Youth Congress recruits when they went out to collect their millions for the party funds. Nobody dared to question them. People's salaries were stopped if they couldn't produce evidence that they were helping in the vasectomy drives; others were put in jail because they had crossed the path of one or the other member of the caucus; homes were raided, women harassed and the torture of detainees continued. It all went on for nineteen months.

And then the monster of fear that she herself had created betrayed her by convincing her that she was still a popular leader. She announced the elections and the flood gates were opened. The vast reality of India pushed Mrs Gandhi, Sanjay and the caucus aside like a fistful of straw. She had spent millions in her election campaign, and it did nothing for her because the people of India were not prepared to have her back. The Janata Party, which was born in the jails during the Emergency, had no money and no time, but was not short of volunteers. The youth of India rallied and came in their thousands to help to overthrow the régime of terror and corruption. But all of this was still largely an unknown quantity to me as I went to interview Mrs Gandhi at her home.

I wondered, as I entered No. 1 Safdar Jung Road, how Mrs Gandhi must feel now. She had been the darling of the people of India from 1966–7 to the early 1970s – the steel of her character much admired, her integrity unquestioned – but then the decline had come. I wondered how she was coping with it. The first time I had seen her was when as a little girl I used to take part in a children's programme on All-India Radio. She had come one autumn morning as the guest of honour. All I remembered of that morning was that she had been very beautiful, and that when she entered the studio all eyes turned and rested on her and that it remained that way throughout the programme. Would the magnetism and the confidence still be there?

I went into the reception room. It looked surprisingly tatty. The carpet was worn, the paint peeling from the walls. There were three people sitting there other than the receptionist. I stood and waited while they tried to find out if I could go in. I looked out of the window, and noticed that the roof of the house had a row of searchlights. I also noticed that an area of lawn had been fenced off and a notice hung there which said 'Beware Guard Dogs'. There was a lot of barbed wire around the outside walls, too. The gate remained shut, and two guards were posted to make sure that the gate was opened only to the few authorized people. There were quite a number of security men around. It surprised me a little, because she was after all now only an ordinary citizen.

Just then the receptionist told me I could go in. I saw Usha Bhagat, Mrs Gandhi's personal secretary, first and persuaded her to let me see Mrs Gandhi. A few minutes later Mrs Gandhi came into the room. I felt foolish at having worried about how she would look, because as she came in – a slender old woman with graceful movements – the room lit up. Her face, a proud, sensitive face, is very like her father's. Her large luminous eyes kept looking as though the tears would spill out of them at any minute. They darted about, and her hands continually fidgeted in her lap. Sometimes she picked up the corner of her sari and twisted it round her fingers again and again. She repeatedly said: 'No matter what I say and how it is put across, they are going to use it against me.'

The hands moved nervously in her lap again. She looked desperately unsure and very afraid. I wondered at that moment if it was possible for her to be afraid. I mean, here we were in the twentieth century, and, after all, she was Nehru's daughter. She shouldn't be afraid sitting in the heart of India. In that moment she looked so like Nehru had done after the Chinese invasion of India. Nehru had felt betrayed, and it had hurt his pride deeply. I could sense the same hurt and pain in Mrs Gandhi. In that moment I so wanted to believe that she was innocent and a victim, that my heart went out to her. I had heard about the Emergency from the world press and from the Indian people, but I hoped to discover how she had been used by her caucus – how the Frankenstein monster had taken over its creator. So I found myself devising ways of writing a book about her which would not endanger her in any way but would at the same time give an insight into the person who is Indira Gandhi. So I suggested a solution.

'Why not let me record a series of conversations with you? In that way I can project a very personal but a very human side of your personality. As long as the book remains my assessment on the basis of these conversations, nobody can accuse you of anything.'

She realized the truth of this immediately and said: 'Yes, I can see that. All right, why don't you tell me the sort of questions you would like to ask. Or better still, perhaps you could type them out and let me have the list. I think it's only after I have seen the questions that I will be able to tell whether I am in a position to answer them.'

I agreed with her and told her that I would bring the questions tomorrow. On the journey back I decided that I would have to find out if my reading of her personality had been right. Had she really been afraid, or was it just a clever bit of acting? I had to find out more about the Emergency, more about what the people thought of her.

I remembered how the press had reacted when Mrs Gandhi had declared the Emergency. The arrests of Jai Prakash Narayan and the other elderly members of the opposition parties had horrified the world. But she had done much that was badly needed. She had banned a number of religious fanatic organizations along with extreme left-wing organizations like the Naxalites.

I too disapproved of the fanatical elements, for they were the reason why India had never become a truly secular state. And the violence of the Marxist Naxalites had been horrifying. Mrs Gandhi had opposed the student agitations and the general lawlessness of India. I too had felt deeply many times that the political student agitations had been organized by frustrated politicians, or else used by the students as an excuse for not appearing in examinations. Very rarely had the students protested about worthwhile things.

I had also felt that the malpractice during her election campaign – which amounted to using her PA to help her – may not have been strictly legal, but was something that most politicians in the world would have done. It had been Mr Raj Narain, her political opponent in her constituency of Rai Bareli, who had brought this court case against her and eventually won it. The decision of the court, when it was announced on 10 June 1975, coincided with the election results from the State of Gujarat. It must have been a terrible blow to lose the court case and at the same time become aware of the absolute victory of the Gujarat students.

The Gujarat students were the first to be successful in this way. They had campaigned against a corrupt Congress State Government, forced the Government to resign and successfully organized the elections so that the Congress Party lost heavily in Gujarat. Mrs Gandhi knew perfectly well that a precedent had been set, and that now it would be only a matter of time before students from other states followed suit.

So I had understood when she had announced the Emergency. I had wished that the rapport between herself and her party members could have been better so that she could have resigned and sorted out the court case. But since she had not given back the power once she had acquired it, it was certain that people wouldn't hand it back to her once she resigned. So the honourable solution, which would also have been the moral one, couldn't be done, and she had opted out for the political solution. I was sad, but I also accepted that, in some ways, if she could control the Emergency and the fear which would stem from it, then it might do the Indian people a lot of good. The Indian press I had little respect for since it really was seldom that they did a responsible job. I knew too many journalists who would write about various countries in the hope of a free trip abroad, or cover some function or other favourably in return for a case of whisky. So really I didn't think that Mrs Gandhi had gagged the press so much as they had already gagged themselves by being afraid of losing their privileges.

There were isolated examples of journalists who had the courage of their convictions and were prepared to go to jail for it, and these had made me feel unhappy about the restrictions. But I felt that if by causing this one loss, the freedom of the press, Mrs Gandhi could stop inflation, rising unemployment and corruption, then as long as there was a time limit on the Emergency, perhaps the price was not too high. But she had been unable to control it. It had gone on for nineteen months, and if what I had been hearing during the past twenty-four hours was anywhere near the truth, then I had to investigate more deeply.

I decided to begin my search immediately. I needed to know the truth. Only in the light of the truth could a book about her have validity.

2 The search for the truth

I began the next day by first drafting the list of those questions that I thought Mrs Gandhi could answer without compromising herself. My list was as follows:

1. You had always been involved in politics in one capacity or the other. What made you decide to take the driving seat?
2. What were the problems about India that you felt most deeply about?
3. When you look back on your eleven years of power, what were the moments when you felt a sense of achievement?
4. What were the disappointments?
5. Did you sometimes feel that things were not moving as fast as you would like them to?
6. Why the Emergency? – Did you feel that years had passed and you were still a long way away from your dreams about India? And that some kind of discipline imposed was the only answer?
7. You were the Prime Minister of the biggest democracy in the world – you had the world at your feet. Did the job carry any disadvantages as well, e.g. loneliness, isolation?
8. If you could put the clock back, what would you like to change most?
9. You are the most important and influential woman in the world for the last fifty years at least. Did it happen easily – naturally? Are you glad that it happened?

10. Or was the price paid too great?
11. Now – yesterday you reminded me so much of something I had
    seen in your father's face after the Chinese Invasion of India.
    Do you feel the same sense of disillusionment?

I hoped that the questions were not to do too directly with Mrs Gandhi the politician. But that, if she chose to answer them truthfully, we would be able to see the political events in the light of her personality. I delivered the questions to Usha Bhagat. Mrs Gandhi herself was out, but I was promised an early reply.

When I got back home I began my research into the atrocities that had been committed during the Emergency. The material was now accumulating thick and fast. But before I go into details, let me describe what happened when the Emergency was declared in June 1975.

There had been much speculation among politicians and journalists as to what Mrs Gandhi would do once Justice Jag Mohan Lal Sinha of Allahabad High Court had given judgement on the petition Mr Raj Narain had filed against the Prime Minister's election to the Lower House of India. The hearing had taken four years, and it ended on 23 May 1975. The judgement was announced on 12 June 1975, and Mrs Gandhi had been unseated as a result. The judge had also debarred her from holding any elected post for six years. This part of the judgement had unnerved not only Mrs Gandhi but each one of her supporters. It would have been one matter if she could have fought an election immediately and come back, but once she had accepted waiting for six years, she would never have been able to come back as Prime Minister. All it would have needed would be for any party members to start a couple of inquiries about her at that time, and that would have been the end. She had been given eighteen days to continue to work till a successor was found. But then she declared with her second son Sanjay that she would under no circumstances resign.

At midnight on 25 June 1975 a series of incidents occurred in various parts of the country. Nobody at first connected them with each other. There were reports from various cities that the streets were full of policemen. There were also reports that a press and all the copies of the newspaper it was printing had been stopped by the police in Jullundhar. There was another report that there was no electricity in any of the newspaper offices in Bahadur Shah Zaffar Marg, which is New Delhi's Fleet Street. There were also rumours of mass arrests of various leaders, including Jai Prakash Narayan, Chandra Shekhar and Mr Morarji Desai. But nobody realized the real implications of what was happening until the next morning. From that moment onwards until 18 January 1977 India would be a dictatorship in which people had lost their right of appeal for wrongful arrest.

Everybody and anybody could be arrested under the DIR (Defence of India Rule) or the MISA (Maintenance of Internal Security Act). Both these pieces of legislation were grossly misused during the Emergency, the first one having been devised for the defence of the borders of India and the second essentially to deal with smugglers and criminals who endangered the internal security of India or committed economic swindles. Mrs Gandhi also employed a vast network of police who could provide a stronger security. She used for this purpose the Border Security Force, the Central Industrial Security Force, Home Guards and the Central Reserve Police, without taking the army into account. She also made use of the Research and an Analysis Wing of the Cabinet Secretariat and Central Bureau of Investigation. It became dangerous to talk freely in India after that morning. Big Brother himself was present and ever-watchful. People were shocked and full of disbelief. They kept trying to find reasons to justify such an act. She realized this and organized massive political rallies in her support so that, in their confused state, the people could be brainwashed into accepting her decision. Later on in the Emergency, she took away powers from the judiciary system itself.

Opposition Parties like the RSS (Rashtriya Swayam Sevak Sangha) and the Jana Sangha and Anand Marg, which were relatively fanatical Hindu organizations, were banned. Along with them all other political parties, including the Marxist Naxalites, were banned, the only exception being the Communist Party of India. This ban extended to include all Mahatma Gandhi-inspired organizations, and the leaders from all these organizations were arrested and put in jail. The press had to submit any report that it wished to publish to the Censor, who carefully deleted any critical remarks about the Government and any photographs of leaders considered dangerous.

Today people were once again free and able to speak, but the shock of the previous nineteen months was not easy to get over. They were only just beginning to feel secure enough to be able to relate their own personal tragedies.

A lot of criticism of Sanjay and Mrs Gandhi had begun to appear in the papers. One incident which kept cropping up was the mysterious Nagarwala 'case'. It had begun six years before on 24 May 1971, and had remained shrouded in mist ever since. Now people were asking questions about it again. When the story first broke, it had caused an enormous public outcry, and two days after it was first known, a very harassed Mr Chavan, then the Finance Minister, had pleaded with the Opposition in the Lower House to stop their questioning, and 'For God's sake not to bring in the name of the Prime Minister.'

According to Mr Chavan, Mrs Gandhi did not have any secret accounts in the State Bank of India. The only two accounts which she could operate were the Jawahar Lal Nehru Memorial Trust Fund and the Sardar Petal Memorial Trust Fund. The Finance Minister had told the Lower House the story as he knew it. He said, 'At about 12.30 p.m. on 24 May 1971 Mr V.P. Malhotra, Chief Cashier of the State Bank of India, drew a sum of 60 lakhs (about £6 million) in hundred-rupee notes from the currency chest of the bank. According to the officer in charge of cash, Mr Malhotra told them that the money was needed for making some large payments.'

He further told the Deputy Head Cashier that he would give him the required form duly filled out. Then a staff car was summoned by him, which he drove himself for a short distance. He was then allegedly met by somebody who drove in the car with him. Later on in the evening, Mr Malhotra had come into the Parliament Street Police Station accompanied by a policeman and reported that he had been the victim of a fraud and that the 60 lakhs of rupees had been taken away in a taxi.

The same night Mr Rustom Sohrab Nagarwala was arrested by Mr K. D. Kashyap, Deputy Superintendent of Police. He was allegedly carrying the entire sum of money, less 5,700 rupees.

Police made a statement and said that Nagarwala had mimicked the Prime Minister's voice over the phone and told Mr Malhotra to draw the money from the bank and hand it over. Mr Malhotra confirmed this, and said, 'She said she needed it for secret help to Bangladesh.'

On 27 May Nagarwala was sentenced to four years' rigorous imprisonment by Mr K. P. Khanna, Judicial Magistrate, New Delhi. Apparently Mr Nagarwala had made a full confession. But about a fortnight later, a Mr Jha, before Mr Justice Dalip K. Kapoor of Delhi High Court, challenged the legality of the proceedings of the State Bank Fraud Case which had led to the conviction of Nagarwala.

On 25 June Nagarwala himself applied to Mr K. S. Sidhu, and said that the confession which led to his conviction had not been voluntary. Then another mysterious thing happened on 13 July – some important documents were reported missing from the case file. The judge, Mr R. N. Agarwal, took a very serious view of these missing documents and on 21 July ordered a re-trial on the grounds that the earlier trial had been held in undue haste, giving rise to a 'miscarriage of justice'.

Following the re-trial, events began to move quickly. On 30 August 1971, Mr Justice P. S. Safeer of the Delhi High Court ordered the immediate sealing of all records of the Lower and Appellate Courts connected with the Nagarwala case. On 20 November Mr K. D. Kashyap, the Deputy Superintendent of Police responsible for the arrest of Nagarwala, died in a car crash while on his honeymoon, and his wife was seriously injured. The other vehicle involved was never found. On 2 March 1972, Nagarwala himself died while still in judicial custody. His death allegedly resulted from cardiac arrest, but opposition leaders described the two deaths as too convenient a coincidence.

To complete the story of the Nagarwala case, all that needs to be said is that several people who had known him well had said that he was prepared to 'unmask' all those connected with the incident. On 30 May 1972, the entire opposition, barring the Communist Party of India, had staged a walkout from the Lower House in protest against Mrs Gandhi's Government's rejection of the demand for an inquiry by a Parliamentary Committee. On 18 November Mr Malhotra who had managed to escape being named as a co-accused in the case was dismissed by the State Bank of India. It was later reported that he had found a fairly powerful job as a financial adviser with Sanjay's Maruti empire.

One more interesting point deserves to be stated: during the re-trial, Nagarwala was reported to have said that soon after he returned from a teaching job in Japan he had a serious accident on the road between Bombay and Poona. This resulted in skull and facial injuries which left him partially paralysed on one side of his face. Mr Maheshwari contended that because of this it would have been impossible for Nagarwala to mimic anyone. He had very little voice left anyhow. No wonder people were demanding an inquiry which would solve the mystery once and for all.

A small leaflet entitled 'Maruti to Mafia' became a bestseller, with its descriptions of the whole history of Sanjay Gandhi's small car factory, Maruti Limited, and the subsequent empire that stemmed from it. But it seems important at this point to tell a little more about Sanjay before going further into Maruti's affairs.

Indira and Feroz Gandhi had two children – Rajiv and Sanjay. The marriage was fairly rocky from the start. She became very involved in running Nehru's household in the newly independent India, and so the children, growing up, had to face the same sort of problem that she herself had faced when small, when her father had been too involved in the Freedom Movement of India to give much time to his growing daughter. Her two children were also sent to a boarding school. The school, the Doon School, Dehra Doon, is a very good one and, in India at least, has a reputation for being the school for the rich.

Sanjay proved to be the child who was always difficult, always unsettled and unsettling. After several turbulent years in Doon School he was eventually expelled. He had an interest in car mechanics, and like the doting mother who believes that because her three-year-old can write a rhyme he will automatically become a famous poet when he grows up, Mrs Gandhi thought that Sanjay must be a mechanical genius. He was sent to England to work as an apprentice in the Rolls-Royce factory. After being convicted for drunken driving, and later fired by Rolls-Royce, who obviously did not consider him a mechanical genius, Sanjay arrived back in India to pick up where he had left off. The whole of his adolescent years had been full of incidents which would appear in the papers, though that was as far as they were allowed to go. Sometimes a car theft was involved, sometimes some other act of hooliganism, and, very often, a girl or two was thrown in for good measure. Sanjay always presented the standard image of the spoiled son of a rich family.

Mrs Gandhi obviously did not share the people's view of Sanjay. From the moment he arrived back from England he began to show interest in attempting to manufacture a small car, around the time when the necessity of a small car for India was being much discussed. The people's small car, made entirely by Indian workmen with parts manufactured entirely in India, was something which had been talked about since 1950. Renault of France had made a particularly good offer, and all the other leading car manufacturers of the world, Volkswagen, Toyota, Citroën and Morris, were keen to collaborate.

Sanjay arrived on the scene long after everybody else had been battling for a considerable time and decided to build a small prototype to show to the public. He built it in the back yard of an old garage in Delhi. This, of course, settled the matter of who the licence would go to, and in November 1970, despite a totally damning criticism of the prototype, a licence was granted to Maruti Limited. Sanjay was to produce 50,000 cars per year. Thus the Maruti Company was formed by Sanjay, and he was its Managing Director, his total shareholding amounting to one share of 100 rupees. Two main things were guaranteed in the letter of intent: first, the car should be built from entirely Indian resources; secondly, it should be low priced.

In retrospect it is very clear that neither of these two promises could possibly have ever been fulfilled. Nevertheless, a door had been opened for Sanjay Gandhi which would enable him to amass a fortune. Mr Bansi Lal, then the Chief Minister of Haryana, in his usual style allocated 445 acres of arable land on the highway that runs between Delhi and Gurgaron. This helpful gesture led to the inhabitants of three villages being evicted from their homes and farms. The price paid to them as token compensation was, of course, far below the market value of the land. Mr Bansi Lal then enabled Sanjay to buy that land at a ridiculously low price, and a government loan was granted to cover it.

The financing of Maruti Limited from that point onwards was easy indeed. There was no shortage of businessmen who would do this sort of favour for the Prime Minister's son when at some future date they could demand a favour in return. Within four years Maruti had acquired a total of 21,891,042 rupees from various dealers placing orders for the non-existent Maruti car. Sanjay was having no success whatsoever with the car design itself. The first one was abandoned, the second didn't work either, and it must really have begun to look quite a bleak prospect to all those involved. But, of course, no doubts were ever stated in public.

It began to look imperative that a working model of the Maruti should be produced. Creditors were beginning to make demands for either the car or their money back. At about this time Mrs Gandhi announced the nationalization of the banks, and as a consequence it became easy to oblige one of the nationalized banks to advance Maruti more money. All such loans were, of course, unsecured, and the Reserve Bank of India eventually insisted that no further loans could be allowed to the company. But by then the Punjab National Bank and the Central Bank of India had each allowed a loan of 7.5 million rupees. Things were beginning to look ominous for Sanjay: inquiries were being demanded. At this point the Allahabad High Court judgement was announced, Mrs Gandhi declared the Emergency and absolute power passed into the hands of mother and son.

Those who had dared to question Sanjay over Maruti were immediately punished, either by being sacked or retired from their jobs. Some months before starting Maruti Limited, Sanjay had started another company. This was Maruti Technical Services Private Limited. Unlike Maruti Limited, it was very much a family concern. Then, later on, there were Maruti Heavy Works Limited and several agencies for foreign concerns that Sanjay acquired. Without the Emergency, none of these companies and agencies would have meant much.

It was the absolute power that Sanjay enjoyed which made it possible for him to make money out of each of his enterprises. If any official questioned why a contract was given to Sanjay, that officer would be sacked. Slowly it became the accepted thing that if Sanjay wanted a particular contract for any one of his companies, then he was allowed it without quibble. The provinces fell over each other to place orders with him, and this was the one kind of flattery he appreciated. Bus bodies were ordered by the hundred, as were road rollers, whether the province or authority needed them or not. According to various sources, from the orders of bus bodies alone Maruti Heavy Vehicles would have made a net profit of 10 million rupees.

The most astounding incident in all these shady deals concerned a water purifier called 'Quick Floc Polymix'. Maruti was a representative for chemicals, telephone cables and bulldozers among other things, and Quick Floc Polymix was manufactured by Maruti Technical Services. It had never been tested by the National Environment and Engineering Research Institute of Kanpur, but despite this Sanjay made a deal with the Municipal Commissioner, Mr B. R. Tamta, to use Quick Floc Polymix in Delhi's water supplies and sewage system instead of the usual filtering processes. In Europe, where this particular product is used, it is only to treat sewage water. But Sanjay used it for everything. Luckily for the citizens of Delhi the Emergency soon ended, otherwise they wouldn't have got away with nothing more than hepatitis outbreaks since the toxic levels which accumulate from this substance can cause various types of skin and eye disease.

It was equally lucky that Sanjay's scheme for a third airline never materialized. He had formed Maruti Aviation Company and acquired agencies not only for Piper Aircraft but also for Maule Aircraft. It is known that he was trying to acquire Safdar Jung Airport. While Sanjay's other companies made vast profits, Maruti Limited unfortunately made a loss of nearly 23 million rupees, which, I suppose, more or less matches its initial paid-up capital of about 26 million. Inquiries into Maruti and all the other companies involved are now going forward. Those involved in working for Sanjay are also facing inquiries into their activities. Time will tell the results, and the results will show whether India has matured as a consequence of her experiences.

This at least gives a glimpse into the corruption on a national scale that was taking place. The terror has yet to be chronicled.

The present Communications Minister, Mr George Fernandes, has been a well-known labour leader for many years, and his battle with Mrs Gandhi was a long one. She had accused him of organizing strikes and subversive activities which were bringing industry to a standstill. His was one of the first names on the list of people to be arrested on the night of 25 June 1975. Luckily for George, he not only suspected that something was afoot, but was warned about his impending arrest. He went underground. The Government, frustrated at not being able to find him, began to harass his family. His brother, Laurence Fernandes, was arrested and beaten up in the hope that he would be able to give away George's whereabouts. After the election results, Laurence Fernandes allowed an interview to be published giving details of his arrest and torture.

And each day a new headline in the newspapers piled on fresh horror as new facts came to light:

'The Murder of the Famous Film Star Sneh Lata Reddy of South India.'

'Another Terrifying Arrest of Dr and Mrs Devnathan in Bombay.'

'The Arrest and Subsequent Death of the Famous Hindi Poet Renu.'

'The Total Disappearance Without Trace of the 23-year-old Civil Engineering Student Rajan from Kerala While He Was in Police Custody.'

'The Seventy-Seven Murders of the so-called Naxalites.'

This last headline referred to the seventy-seven *known* murders, for it is believed that there were many more in such provinces as Andhra, West Bengal, Kerala, Bihar and Orissa. The Naxalites are, of course, on the extreme left wing of the Communist Party, and are pro-Maoist. In Bengal, at least for a while, they had terrorized the population by killing anybody whom they considered to be a capitalist and by any means which they considered fit. But during the Emergency, under the banner of killing Naxalites or arresting so-called left-wingers, many innocent people were killed or arrested. Such things could happen at any time in a totally personal family feud between a policeman's family and a civilian. The civilian had no rights, the policeman had the power, and the rest is history.

An inquiry was demanded into Jai Prakash Narayan's treatment while in custody in Chandigarh to decide whether his kidneys had been deliberately damaged.

Several reports about Mr Bansi Lal appeared in the *Hindustan Times*, the *Indian Express* and the *Times of India* in the month of May 1977. He had been Defence Minister in Mrs Gandhi's Cabinet, and a close friend of both Mrs Gandhi and Sanjay. In fact, he was said to be the real power behind Sanjay. According to the report, Bansi Lal had made life hell for an additional sessions judge who had refused to decide against Mr Ram Piara, one of his political opponents. Mr Ram Piara himself made statements about what happened to him. He was detained under the Maintenance of Internal Security Act in 1974 on a charge of trying to topple the Bansi Lal Ministry. In 1975, his two sons were also arrested under the Defence of India Rule. During the Emergency, anyone arrested under either of these Acts could be held indefinitely without trial. In fact, the case passed out of the hands of the judiciary the moment a person was charged under either. Mr Ram Piara's house was also raided repeatedly. The police knocked at the door every night at two or three in the morning and harassed the female members of his household. Eventually the family fled to another town, Karnal.

Reports also began to appear about Sanjay and Mr V. C. Shukla and other Ministers having VIP suites permanently available in Delhi's five-star hotels. The food and drink were mostly organized by the hotel, while the women were organized by grateful clients.

The film industry complained that the Minister of Information and Broadcasting, Mr V. C. Shukla, had given specific instructions about how a film would be passed by the Board of Censors: the names of actresses required to visit Mr Shukla before the film was allowed to be shown to the public were given to the producer in advance.

An inquiry against Mr Jag Mohan, Vice-Chairman of Delhi Development Authority, was announced for misuse of power, corrupt methods and profiteering. Mr Jag Mohan had been Sanjay's right-hand man in the 'Clean Delhi Campaign'.

A newspaper requested that an inquiry should be held into the death of Mr Fakhruddin Ahmad, the President of India. It was rumoured that the President had been visited by Mrs Gandhi, Mr Bansi Lal and Sanjay the night before his death. One of the chauffeurs of the President, who happened to be passing the room where the group were, is said to have overheard loud arguments between Sanjay and the President. It was alleged that he also heard thumping noises. Later on in the night the President suffered a heart attack and died. His wife remained silent except for one moment when, in a deeply distressed voice, she reportedly said, 'Zalimo Ne Unhe Mar Dala.' (In literal translation, 'Those cruel people, they have killed him.') Mrs Gandhi has consistently denied that she went to see the President on the fatal night.

Mrs Ahmad has also remained quiet. What is interesting is the fact that Dr Chug, who made out the death certificate for the President, was travelling with his wife and their children in their car a week after the President's death. An army truck appeared and crashed into them so violently that every member of the family was killed. Yet the movement of this mysterious army truck was never recorded. Everyone at Army Headquarters flatly denies that an army truck was in the area on the day in question.

It is amazing how a similar fate repeatedly eliminated potential witnesses in cases connected with Mrs Gandhi, Sanjay or Bansi Lal. In the course of talking to various senior officials in the Government of India, I asked one whether there was going to be an inquiry into Mrs Gandhi's conduct. The gentleman smiled and said, 'How can there be? There are never any witnesses left alive.' The sentence sent a shudder down my spine. For a moment I wasn't sure whether we were talking about the Prime Minister of India or a common mafia Don.

The papers also made a lot about Dhirendra Brahmachari, a personal friend and yoga teacher of Mrs Gandhi: his private aeroplane, his huge ashram in Delhi and another in Kashmir, and the incidents surrounding them. A report in the *Times of India* described his whim in September 1975 to own a black cross-bred Jersey cow. Swami Dhirendra Brahmachari is an interesting figure. He has been involved with the Nehru family since the days when Nehru was still alive, and Mrs Gandhi has always had a soft spot for him. In the days of the Emergency, the Swami took full advantage of this weakness, and when Bansi Lal was informed of the desire of the Swami for a black Jersey cow, he sent his henchmen from the Haryana police in search of such an animal. Eventually they found such a creature in the town of Jagadhri. Even its eyes, tongue, horns and hoofs were black. The cow was a valuable possession, since she also had an equally black calf and was yielding plenty of milk. Cow and calf were both taken to the Swami's ashram in Kashmir. The Swami liked the cow, and directed the truck driver who had brought them to take them straight back to Delhi to the Swami's ashram there. The truck driver was lucky as he was paid petrol charges. The owner of the cow had never received anything.

The 'Clean Delhi Campaign' had begun to come in for a lot of criticism. One incident in particular, which became known as

'The Turkman Gate Affair', featured largely in the newspapers. Sanjay had had a thing about wanting to clear the shanty-towns from Delhi, and his obsession to clean Delhi at whatever cost led him to the shanty-town outside the city wall of Old Delhi. It is barely four miles from the Prime Minister's residence. Evidently he gave an ultimatum to the poor people who lived there, but since the only alternative accommodation they had been offered did not even have a water supply, they had refused to leave. On the final day Sanjay arrived with bulldozers and ordered the mud huts to be razed. The official casualty figures are seventeen people dead and 200 injured, some very seriously. The unofficial figure runs into well over 100 dead and 700 injured. All the casualties were inside their homes when the incident took place.

The so-called 'opposition leaders' arrested during the Emergency included thousands of social workers who belonged to the Mahatma Gandhi-inspired organizations. Their only crimes had been to work and help in the development of the remote villages of India. If all the people arrested were a danger to India's security, then how did it come about that they included disciples of Mahatma Gandhi?

The press reported widely on Sanjay's various girl friends, including Rukhsana Sultana and Ambika Soni, and the power these women had wielded. Ambika Soni was the President of the Youth Congress in the days when the Youth Congress acquired as its members every hoodlum and petty gangster in Delhi, who were then used to terrorize people into collecting money for the Youth Congress. Rukhsana Sultana was behind the vasectomy drive, and is said to have been responsible for 15,000 vasectomies herself.

An official of the State Government of Rajasthan told me a sad tale from a village near Muzaffar Nagar. An old man came and killed a doctor, his assistant and the block development officer with a knife one evening. He didn't run away, but just waited to be arrested. When questioned, the old man wept and said, 'These people performed vasectomy on my only son today. My son had been married one month, and now the family name will not live after my son. I don't mind if I hang for the murder of those who caused it.'

The village of Riwasa in Haryana refused to have vasectomies performed on its male population. Swords were drawn and a riot

34

followed when the authorities refused to listen.

It seemed that every day new inquiries were being held or demanded about the conduct of Ministers in Mrs Gandhi's Cabinet and the Chief Ministers of various provinces who were her special favourites. The terrorizing of the general population by members of Sanjay's Youth Congress was another thing about which people were openly demanding that something be done. In other words, misuse of power by government officials or influential people was the main target. A friend of mine has a nephew who has a shop in the Old City of Delhi. I went to have dinner with them while I was there. He told me how Sanjay and his men had demanded that each and every shop in this famous old street called the Chaori Bazaar should donate 7,000 rupees apiece or the bulldozers would move in under the 'Clean Delhi Campaign' and the street would be bulldozed. All had paid.

I had still heard nothing about Mrs Gandhi's reactions to my questions. So I decided to try and find out who among her friends would be willing to talk about her, not as a politician but as a friend. People in power don't have many friends, but they usually have some. But in her case I couldn't find anyone willing to talk about her as a friend. Is it possible that people were afraid of the present Government, or that they were afraid of her coming back to power one day? But I wasn't looking for dirt. I really wanted to know what made her tick. I really wanted to know what kind of human being she is. I took care to make it very clear to whoever I went to see that this was the case, but only those who wanted to attack her were willing to talk, and these were mostly members of the press or of the present Government.

Delhi has long used two phrases to describe the two sorts of groups of men and women who clustered around Mrs Gandhi. I don't know which newspaper or hurt friend first coined the phrase, but the more influential group around her was supposed to constitute the 'Bedroom Cabinet', while the slightly lesser beings were known as the 'Kitchen Cabinet'. One of the reasons that I was given for her lack of friends was that she changed her 'Bedroom Cabinet' too frequently. As a result, she hurt too many people. Another was that she was unable to give affection.

While I am not sure whether the terms 'Bedroom Cabinet' or

35

'Kitchen Cabinet' were invented in vengeance, I do know that Mrs Gandhi always had her favourites. Bright, good-looking men, brought into the limelight suddenly, were given enormous power and influence. These men would rise to incredible heights and then lapse into obscurity when someone else was picked out and given the same treatment. When in favour, they had the world at their feet; when fallen from grace, they were never heard of again.

The names of such men is common knowledge among all those who know Indian politics. I was told that the two-tier cabinet in her house had the following names in it, to take the more influential ones first (those with asterisks were with her till the end):

*Mohammad Yunus, *Yash Pal Kapur, *R. K. D. Dhavan,

Dhirendra Brahmachari, *Sidhartha Shankar Ray, *Bansi Lal,

*Om. Mehta, Dr Karan Singh, V. C. Shukla.

The names of those with less influence were as follows:

D. P. Mishra, Dinesh Singh, Nandini Satpathy, Teji Bachchan.

Most members of the more influential part of the caucus around her have been among those recently arrested. Bail has been allowed for them, but inquiries and court cases are proceeding, the charges against them involving 'misappropriation of party funds and misuse of authority'. Details of the charges have not yet been made public, but it is stated that the misappropriation of party funds and the syphoning of them into non-existent private companies alone amounts to six million pounds of the funds from the Congress Party of India, and four million pounds of funds belonging to the Youth Congress.

In the end, Mrs Gandhi contacted me through her secretary Usha Bhagat. I was told that she had some reservations about the questions. I suggested that I call on her again to try and explain how I intended to handle them, and was allowed to see her the following morning.

This was during the early hours between 8.30 a.m. and 10 a.m. when she always sees whoever calls on her. I was told that many people still came to offer her their support and to beg her to sort out some official problem or other. It was interesting to watch this happening before I was allowed to see her myself, but then I witnessed an illustration of that 'coldness' which people had mentioned to me about her.

An old man had travelled a hundred miles or so just to see her. He had no bundle of files that he wanted her to do something about, but said that he only wanted to see her to tell her that his family would forever remain loyal to the Nehrus. He became quite emotional, and said, 'I have fought behind your father and I will die for you.' As the tears rolled down the old man's craggy face and he tried to reach out to touch her feet, she recoiled from his touch. A mask came over her face and she said, in a detached sort of way, 'All right, all right. Now leave it.' And she moved away from the perplexed old man, little realizing the damage she had done. She had felt uneasy over the old man's show of affection, and had remained unmoved by it. I wondered if the old man would ever come back, or, indeed, vote for her if she ever decided to stand in elections again.

She had very little time to spare for me that morning, but as far as I could understand it she didn't believe that my questions could remain non-political. She also said that she wasn't sure how far she could really trust me. I tried to reassure her and she promised to think about it a bit more. I came away with a strange feeling that the only way she would feel sure about what I wrote would be by paying me herself. She hadn't yet mentioned it in so many words, but I had that impression. Anyway, she promised to see me again in two days' time to let me know her decision.

By now I had convinced myself that I did indeed need to probe more deeply to find out whether all the random reports in the newspapers told of isolated incidents or of planned and organized acts in violation of the honour of the Indian masses and all leading back to the 'fountainhead of corruption', Mrs Gandhi.

The first case that I decided to investigate was that of a young man of twenty-three who had been a student of the Civil Engineering College in Cochin and who had been missing since March 1976. His father, Professor Eachara Warrier, had knocked at the doors of virtually every jail in the area, but nobody had been able to tell him anything about his son. Apparently the young man, whose name was Rajan, had been arrested along with another called Joseph Challey at half past five on the morning of 3 March 1976. They were taken from the students' lodging house, and their parents knew nothing about it for twenty-four hours. As soon as he heard, Professor Warrier began to search for his only son. All he knew was that his son had asked for a glass of water as they were being bundled into a police van and he had been given water by one of the other young men in the lodging house. Later Professor Warrier also found out that his son had been beaten quite severely until he became unconscious. But that was where the shutters had closed, and no matter how hard the poor professor tried, nobody could or would tell him what had become of his son. He eventually started a lawsuit in the Supreme Court of India, but this was a last desperate plea since the Divisional Bench of Kerala High Court had already given a judgement against him.

The case interested me, and I decided to follow it up. I went to Cochin to meet Professor Warrier. Two days before I arrived, Joseph Challey, the student arrested at the same time as Rajan, had been freed, and I was also able to see him at his home just outside the town.

Kerala provided a strange setting in which to hear about a sinister crime committed by the police. It is a part of India where, legend has it, Christianity is older than in Europe. It is said that St Thomas came to Kerala 2,000 years ago, and it has a Jewish community which dates back to the same period. It is the part of India where the literacy rate is highest, and is where the first Communist government of any Indian state came to power. Its people are educated, mellow and soft-spoken. It is a land of lakes, palm trees, silver sands and old churches, and the rice fields are lush and green. Simple, hospitable people, tiny old-fashioned towns, small villages which are incredibly clean. When I asked what was the produce of Kerala, I was told that it produced cashew nuts, black pepper, cadamums and coconuts, to name but a few. The crops somehow sounded as delicate as the scenery which stretched before me.

Kerala has always been a stronghold of Communism in some form or other. This is always attributed to the fact that, because people are literate here, they are more aware of the contrasts between the unemployed and poor and the rich and influential. The extreme left-wing Naxalites also flourished here. Though the Naxalites had mellowed somewhat with age, they still seemed less than careful over the means to be used to rectify what they considered wrong in society. It was therefore ironic that they should become a banned organization, and that this should be done by a government which also did not care what means it used so long as the end result was the one required.

Once the Emergency was declared and the police given absolute power, then the hunt for anybody who might have been involved in any capacity with the Naxalite movement began in earnest. Both Rajan and Joseph Challey had fallen victim to the same hunt. Neither were involved in politics at all, left wing or otherwise, but they were suspected of having friends who were Naxalites. This was enough reason for their arrest.

The police wanted to know the whereabouts of a couple of Naxalites in their class who were on the run. Rajan and Joseph explained that there were fifty-two young men in their class, and that it would be difficult for them to know the movements of them all. The police refused to listen to them and they were bundled into the van. It was only by the determination of a fellow student in the boarding house that Joseph and Rajan had a glass of water each on that fateful morning. According to Joseph, it was Rajan's last drink, because he died the same night under torture, and it was the last drink Joseph had for the next four days. According to Joseph, they were taken straight to a special torture place, which was not a police station or a jail. Some government guest houses in particularly isolated areas were used for the torture of political detainees, and Joseph and Rajan were taken to one such place.

Joseph said it was dark and bare except for essential torture instruments and a couple of chairs. He and Rajan were made to lie on two wooden benches at either end of a small square room. They were then tied to each bench, and two wooden rods about 8 to 10 inches in diameter were brought to them. Each rod was placed on their chests, and four police constables came to stand on each side of the two benches. They then sat down on each end of the wooden rods as they rested across the chests of the young men. As the rolling of the rods began, the policemen kept their weight on the ends of the rods which they rolled up and down the bodies of the two boys. Both suffered from broken ribs. Then several other kinds of beatings began. They would beat them on the soles of their feet for a while, and then begin the roller treatment again. Both young men were punched repeatedly.

After several hours Rajan became unconscious. One of the policemen said, 'Look at him, he's shamming, I'll soon fix him.' With his boots on, the constable jumped on Rajan's chest and stomach. Rajan stopped breathing at the same time as Joseph became unconscious. According to Joseph, he stayed in a state of semi-consciousness for three days, and he was beaten throughout those three days. The police stopped only when they themselves got tired of beating their prisoner. Three days later, when Joseph came to, he asked a policeman about Rajan. The answer was, 'Oh him, he died that night.'

It was the last Joseph Challey heard of Rajan. His own imprisonment lasted a whole year, and he was released long after the Emergency had been lifted. It was generally believed that Joseph was not released immediately after the elections because he knew what had happened and would certainly talk about it. People involved in the killing were nervous, so they thought the easiest thing would be to keep Joseph in jail as long as possible.

I asked Joseph what he thought he ought to do about it now. His answer was quite simple. 'My parents think that it would be foolish for me to start anything now, they think that I ought to just get on and finish my engineering work. Once I have got my degree and am settled in a job, all this will become like a bad dream. My parents think that if I try to name the people involved in this, then nothing really will happen to the police, only our family will be black-marked and harassed. Not only that, but the police themselves can start a vendetta because this is a small town. I have decided just to finish my exams.'

I was disappointed, but I understood. This thin, frightened young man had no other way. On my way back, I stopped at Professor Warrier's. His is a tiny house and its garden backs on to a railway line. The old man was sitting in a traditional cane chair. He insisted that a cup of tea or coffee be brought, and then we began the interview. Professor Warrier is a thin balding man, who used to teach Hindi in the local college. I asked him if his wife was going to join us. He explained that it was not really possible as she was suffering from such shock since Joseph Challey's release, when all their hopes of seeing Rajan had been finally dashed, that she had become entirely incoherent.

This tired old man, with enormous eyes constantly brimming with tears, now has no son and is doomed to spend the last days of his life with an unbalanced wife.

'You know, Rani, when I began my search for my son I thought, one day I will find him. As the months went on, I began to get suspicious that they had probably broken his limbs so badly that he is a cripple. But I thought, never mind, maybe he will be crippled but I will have my son back. Then, when the rumours of other people being beaten to death began to reach my ears, I hardened myself and I thought that maybe Rajan is dead and all I will have will be possibly the remains of his body. Now I am told that they burnt his body because they did not think that they ought to leave any incriminating evidence. So now I cannot even hope for the remains of his body to enable me to perform his last rites.'

His face crumpled up completely, and he was really crying. I, too, cried for the young twenty-three-year-old who would have looked after his parents in their old age. I also cried for my country where the police are capable of such a brutal murder.

'Every time I drink a glass of water I remember that my one and only son died begging for a few drops of water in this same country of ours where to give water to a thirsty man is one of the noblest of deeds and where the refusal to give someone a glass of water is the greatest sin. I find I can't take a sip from my glass without choking. We can't make special foods on festival days because he who was my stick for the blindness of old age will never again be able to eat any of it. Every time I see a policeman walking down the road I wonder if he was a party to the beating of my son.'

'Do you think, Professor, that there is any way that you can think of which would prevent this senseless killing of your son from being forgotten?'

'Yes, there is, and that is the only reason I am alive. I am going to keep on fighting and keep on knocking on every door to make sure that no father in this country loses his Rajan ever again. I want to go to every school, every college, every university and tell them of my Rajan, so the boys and the girls who are the future of my country never allow such a thing to happen again. It is the only thing that will stop his life from having been wasted.'

I took both the old man's shrivelled-up, trembling hands into mine and said, 'Good luck, I hope you succeed. I am sorry the words are so inadequate. The only tangible thing that I can offer is that if you succeed in making this contact with the young men and women throughout India, you will have acquired yourself not one but thousands of Rajans.'

The old man smiled, a watery, pale smile, and said, 'Yes, I know.'

41

I came away from his house emotionally drained. A thought kept constantly recurring to me: how can we stop it? How can we organize the youth so well that there is never again any possibility of us lapsing into this kind of situation.

I went to a meeting organized by some students, and even more hair-raising incidents came to light. A dozen or so housewives had marched to the centre of the town to demand that their innocent husbands and children be released. A dozen women don't really make a threatening procession. Nevertheless the police used the batons and 'lathis' on them. (A lathis is a stick with a leaded end, normally six and a half feet long.) Some of these women were at this meeting and told me they had all suffered broken bones. Some had got off lightly, with only a broken leg or arm, but some had had their ribs broken and others had had their head split open.

One young man at the meeting pointed out that a lathi charge on women was something that even the British hadn't had the courage to allow. Another student told me of a story about a group of young men from the university. They were arrested under the same ploy of being suspected Naxalites. They were beaten up and then, when the police found that the men really had no information that they could give them, were taken twenty miles into the jungle between Cochin and Trivandram. This jungle has wild elephants in it. The young men had nothing on but pairs of shorts. They didn't even have a stick, let alone a torch. Three days later a news item appeared in the paper about the bodies of four men being found on the road between Trivandram and the jungle. They appeared to have been trampled to death by elephants.

Each one of these young men was somebody's son, somebody's brother, somebody's nephew, lovingly brought up, carefully looked after until the night when the police abandoned them in the jungle. Their only crime was that they did not possess the information the police wished to get out of them. The punishment they unwittingly received was the one reserved for high treason in medieval times.

My visit to Cochin had been organized by Mr Ram Chandran Potti, of the local Serva Seva Sangha. Serva Seva Sangha is a Mahatma Gandhi-inspired organization. It was put into operation immediately after India's Independence when Gandhi decided that the Congress Party had done its duty and should now be disbanded. The main task that Serva Seva Sangha, like all the other

Gandhi-inspired organizations, had decided to tackle was to go down to the grass roots and develop the village.

Mrs Gandhi had considered all such organizations to be a danger to the internal security of India, and had put thousands of their social workers in jail. I was so shocked when I heard this that I had insisted on attending the All-India Conference of Serva Seva Sangha in Bombay. There I met Mr Potti and discovered that he was heading the Committee for the Defence of Rajan. He'd also arranged for a fund to be collected so that Rajan's father could continue to fight in the courts. A poor professor of Hindi in a small college in Cochin doesn't have unlimited resources. My interest in the Rajan case led me to contact Mr Potti, and he, being kindness itself, had arranged my trip.

While in Cochin I stayed at the house of Mr Abraham, a gentle, kindly man who is a devout Christian and a firm believer in J. P. Narayan's Movement Towards Total Revolution. After the success of the Gujarat students' movement, J. P. Narayan had decided in his own mind that youth power, properly controlled, was the answer. At the same time he realized that he needed a net-work of mature social workers who could control the youth organizations. At this point the Mahatma Gandhi-inspired organizations stepped in to offer an already existing network precisely of this nature. They had in any case all worked in close liaison during Vinoba Bhave's land reform movement, and so it was not such a strange step.

At the Conference in Bombay, the Serva Seva Sangha made a major decision. The point in question was whether to dissolve the Sangha now and form a new organization with a complete hierarchy of newly elected people to work under J. P. Narayan's blessing, or to stay as they were. Many felt that if the Sangha stayed as it was, it might disintegrate after J. P. Narayan's death. Perhaps they had seen the deterioration in the Congress Party after Gandhi's death, and later after Nehru's death. I myself feel it would have been better to have dissolved the Sangha then and to have formed a new organization to run the programme of Total Revolution. But the majority vote remained behind keeping the Sangha. J. P. Narayan's People's Committees were to be formed, and the Gandhi-inspired organizations were to help to form them and to train new social workers out of Jai Prakash's youth power.

J. P. Narayan became a voice in the wilderness of India under

Mrs Gandhi as far back as 1969. His perceptive mind was quick to assess that she was leading the country towards dictatorship. But, at that time, he himself was very undecided about how to prevent any of this from happening, and so he remained, so to speak, as the voice of the conscience of the people of India. And Mrs Gandhi became more and more angry about his continuing opposition to her policies. After the declaration of Emergency, when J. P. Narayan too had found the path he was destined to take, things became really impossible. He was either in jail and out of the way, or he was out on parole having his life made very difficult. During one such period he had visited Kerala, and Mrs Gandhi announced that Jai Prakash must not be allowed to stay at any of the government-owned hotels or guest houses. My host in Kerala, Mr Abraham, had offered his home to Jai Prakash. The first thing that I was told when I entered his guest room was that I was to sleep on the bed that Jai Prakash had slept on during his last visit. It was odd to hear a successful businessman talking about being a fervent believer in the Gandhian philosophy and J. P. Narayan's Total Revolution.

Narayan's charisma is such as to have united totally diverse factors in Indian political life. Rashtriya Swayam Sevak Sangha is an essentially Hindu organization, and has been Hindu to such an extent in the past that it has had a reputation for being fanatical. It was at one time accused of being involved in the murder of Mahatma Gandhi, but was later totally exonerated. It has a highly disciplined force of voluntary workers, who form an efficient network and are an influential section of today's ruling Janata Party. Jana Sangha is another similar organization, which is slightly less organized and a little less fanatical besides lacking in discipline. But again it is essentially a Hindu organization.

These two Hindu groups then joined hands with a purely Moslem organization called Jamaat-I-Islami, and with them eventually merged the Socialist Party and the old Congress Party to form the ruling Janata Party. Several other smaller factions from the Indian political scene also united under the Janata flag. Even the left-wing Naxalites have given an undertaking to work according to Ghandian principles. Jai Prakash discovered that the strict discipline that any religious organization demands of its members makes for hard-working social workers, and today, all over India, local leaders of Rashtriya Swayam Sevak Sangha,

Jana Sangha and Jamaat-I-Islami have become important members of the community. As key figures they will liaise between the ruling Janata Party and Jai Prakash's network of People's Committees.

Now, in Cochin, I needed to see all these different leaders. Ever since I had met Rajan's father, I felt very deeply that a way must be found to keep the enthusiasm of the people alive and to stop the Congress Government of the State continuing its corrupt practices. Kerala was one of those states where state elections had been held at the same time as the general elections. It had been a clever move, since, had the result of the national elections come in earlier, the existing Congress Party would perhaps not have been able to bully the electorate into voting for it. But their story is that they were so sure of Mrs Gandhi's victory that there was no point in waiting for the national results to come in.

It had of course had an unfortunate effect on cases such as Rajan's because guilty individuals had retained power. The Central Government wished to intervene and hold an inquiry into the Rajan incident, but the State Government announced that it would hold an inquiry itself. For a while it looked as though justice would not after all be done. But the mood of the people was very determined, and eventually Mr Karuna Karan, the Chief Minister, resigned over the Rajan case. The new Chief Minister, Mr K. Anthony, has now taken over. The Deputy Inspector General of Police was arrested later in May 1977 and charged with Rajan's murder.

Mr Abraham introduced me to all the local party leaders, and I wanted to know what their plans were for the future. Their answers seemed remarkably close to the answers of the Congress leaders after India's Independence, for it seemed to them that the end of the Emergency was an end in itself. The Congress leaders of long ago had also forgotten that self-government does not mean merely getting rid of the foreign power; that it also meant developing each and every individual's ability to govern himself. This must involve giving him the right education, socially, morally, politically and spiritually. Only then can true self-government be achieved. The party leaders sitting before me didn't seem to realize that the problem had not been how to get rid of Mrs Gandhi, but how to stop the same thing happening again.

The same bumbling attitude became apparent through all my

research. People seemed to have no clear vision of what would make the overthrow of Mrs Gandhi a real success. India seems to suffer from this indecision throughout history. The Moslem invasions of India began in A.D. 904 and continued for the next five hundred-odd years until the Moguls decided to settle. And the English came and stayed for two hundred years. And we were never able to unite enough to oppose and rid ourselves of them until Mahatma Gandhi.

It seemed to me that even the Kerala students, given that they had all the enthusiasm of the world, were unable to organize their thoughts enough to formulate a programme for the future. They seemed unaware that it is youth that holds the destiny of India in its hands. It does no good at all to blow up trains or burn buses or hold strikes. All this would only earn them a bad name. What they need is a detailed plan, worked out with meticulous care, which will register protest against the corrupt régime and yet remain constructive in its aims.

The Gujarat students' movement came very close to this ideal. Jai Prakash had led them and they had listened. Excepting one or two isolated incidents of violence, and despite damning propaganda by Mrs Gandhi's Government, the movement had remained peaceful. Curfew was imposed and people were told that all was chaos and danger, but I talked to people who had been closely involved with the movement and their verdict was very favourable. Narayan Desai gave me a particularly objective view of how organized the students had been. I told all this to the students in Kerala, and they sat and listened with the intense concentration of someone who is eager for a glint of light at the far end of the tunnel.

During my flight back to Delhi, as I looked down on the silvery lakes and the fluttering palm trees, I thought of the distress that this one investigation had caused me and the despair still clinging to my person like wet clothes. I hoped very much that somewhere, somehow, all this energy and enthusiasm could be guided in the right direction.

While in Kerala I had acquired a growing certainty that underneath all the gruesome details lay a solid truth. People had said to me in Kerala that it was just luck that Rajan happened to be

46

arrested with another boy who was alive. It was also luck that he had a father who was a literate man, well able to understand the various legal issues and to make use of them. There were many, many more whose fate would probably never be found out since somebody would have already informed the parents in some remote village or other that their son had died of some illness. After all, if I had to work hard and worry all day long about whether I would have enough food to feed my children at the end of the day, then I certainly would not have the means to rush off to a town three or four hundred miles away to look for a dead son. It would be far more convenient to believe what the authorities chose to tell me and to mourn and weep for a few days. How heartbreakingly simple it is to beat somebody's son to death and never be caught or punished.

When I arrived back in Delhi I began my investigations into the Turkman Gate affair. It seemed that it had been on Sanjay Gandhi's orders that the bulldozers moved in. Apparently he had stood by personally and watched as the bulldozers 'cleaned up Delhi'. The casualty figures have already been quoted (see page 29). It seems that someone at the crucial moment rushed to inform Mrs Gandhi about what was happening, and she had immediately driven down and stopped the massacre, but by that time, of course, the story was over.

When I went to India to begin my research I had felt much sympathy for Mrs Gandhi, because I have myself occasionally felt very fascistic when facing India's problems. The slowness of the remedies can lead one to feel throughly exasperated. Cleaning Delhi is very important, and cleaning India is very important, but when you bulldoze down someone's home because you believe that it looks ugly, then you do not do so without giving him alternative accommodation and work. The same kind of thoughtlessness seems to have gone into the vasectomy drive. I doubt very much if anybody really wants to have dozens of children, particularly if there is no money to feed them. But we need to take into account a man's traditions, beliefs and fears. For hundreds of years men have believed that they are not virile enough if they cannot produce children. It isn't as though the men of ancient times did not enjoy sex, but somehow it always included the thought of producing children, and to tell a man he was barren was worse than saying he was impotent. In a poor country like India, having children is also an economic need. The more sons you have, the greater your security in your old age. So it is rather obvious that, to get a man's cooperation, you have to prove to him that a belief thousands of years old is totally without foundation. It is also impossible to understand how orders could ever have been given to round up every male member of a village to be sterilized without any thought being given to age, family circumstances and so forth.

The scare of vasectomy, and the resulting fear of official doctors, became so great, and people so confused, that in one incident where a boys' school had the annual vaccination done to every pupil, a mob of angry parents descended. Vaccination and vasectomy became one and the same in the minds of the people. The fact that the boys had only had an injection seemed to make no difference because of the already existing mistrust of official doctors. In a country like India, where we need desperately to break the barrier that exists between the black Sahib and the villager, such a situation can do untold damage. For years to come, men may well refuse to go to government clinics for fear of sterilization.

I also find it incredible to see Mrs Gandhi sit for a television interview and say with a straight face that all such horrors were initiated by a few over-zealous officials. For I know that my brother, who is a government official, was so harassed and threatened with loss of pay and privileges in countless ways that he had little alternative but to go on the vasectomy drives.

Another friend, who works in Delhi as a teacher, did not receive her salary for three months and was told that they would continue to withhold her salary unless she found ten male or female cases for sterilization. She told me of visiting women's hospitals and eventually finding two mothers who had already been sterilized. She then had to pay them 500 rupees each to sign the form which said that their sterilization was done only because she had persuaded them. She then took these two certificates to her principal and pleaded that she couldn't produce any more because she was quite ill; and with a lot of humming and hawing her salary was eventually released. Similar stories are told by everybody in India. I only quote those which I verified myself.

Nobody has any authority to withhold the salary of a Government of India employee unless the directive comes from the Government itself. It also has to come from heights which can't be questioned.

I went back to see Mrs Gandhi, and she still hadn't made up her mind. Still she worried about some foreign publisher paying me. I was beginning to realize the truth of what my father had said the day I arrived in India. I didn't see now how she could possibly answer any questions truthfully. Whether she pleaded ignorance, or pleaded that she did know about it, either way she was condemning herself as the Prime Minister of the largest democracy in the world. If she didn't know, she was incompetent; if she did know, she was corrupt. The choice was an interesting one. I couldn't quite see which one she would take. I imagined she would keep me hanging around for a while.

Just at that point Delhi decided to have a freak rainstorm. I had received a telephone call from the Gandhi Peace Foundation to say they had a very interesting report that they were about to release to the press and would I like to come and see it? I immediately grabbed a taxi and was on my way when, in a sky that was white with heat, clouds began to gather as the bright afternoon became dark.

Somewhere deep inside me stirred memories of my childhood when, in my father's house, I had stood for hours watching the purple rain-clouds pouring their heart out on the earth. As I sat in the taxi I held my breath with the hope of seeing the thunder and the serpent lightning across the sky again. The anticipation made my skin tingle. Slowly the dark sky developed a film of bright yellow, and for a few minutes everything became fluorescent Then the dust storm unleashed its fury, bending the trees double, scattering the birds from the sky and making my taxi driver terrified. It lasted only a few minutes – a part of the ritual of the rains at this time of the year when the earth is very dry, and each day a little more dust gathers in the sky until eventually there is a dust storm and nature decides to cleanse the atmosphere with a massive cloudburst. After the storm had cleared, the yellow slowly blew away to some distant plains and suddenly the serpent lightning lit up the sky. The colours were unbelievable. It was so sensual, this rain in the middle of the hot afternoon, that I could feel the pleasure of the thirsty trees, plants and grass. The peacocks came out to dance by the roadside. The earth smelled sweet and the fragrance was so joyful that it passed through me and I too felt at peace.

The taxi pulled up at the Gandhi Peace Foundation. The place was teeming with journalists. I was ushered to one side and Mr Radha Krishna, Secretary to the Peace Foundation, handed me a report. He said: 'We were having to be very cautious before we released this report, we needed to be sure that the eye-witnesses will not get into trouble. We have only just brought them in to safety. We also would like to be very sure that a State Inquiry is not allowed to happen in this case. The Central Government must announce an inquiry straight away.'

The report, prepared by the Civil Rights Committee, stated:

> In certain states like Andhra, West Bengal, Kerala, Bihar, Orissa reports have been released to the press that some Naxalites – the extreme leftists – have been killed during 'encounters with the police'. But now there are eye-witnesses who are willing to state that they were in fact murders committed by the police.
>
> As far as Andhra is concerned, on a rough count based on government statements and statements made by the accused in various conspiracy cases in the courts, it would seem that 77 citizens are claimed to have been killed in 'encounters' in Andhra alone during the Emergency. There is widespread apprehension that the 'encounters' were staged, that in fact the citizens have been liquidated in cold blood by the police to terrorize potential dissenters in the state.

On learning about these apprehensions in April 1977, J. P. Narayan, as President of the Citizens for Democracy, set up a committee headed by V. M. Tarkunde to collect evidence about the deaths in Andhra. The committee was carefully chosen and consisted of professors, journalists and economists. Apart from Mr Tarkunde, its members were Nabakrishna Chowdhury (Angul, Orissa), M. V. Ramamurti (Hyderabad), Kaloji Narayan Rao (Warangal), B. G. Verghese, a leading journalist from Delhi, Balwanth Reddy (Hyderabad), K. Pratap Reddy (Hyderabad), K. G. Kannabiran (Hyderabad) and Arun Shourie, a World Bank official residing in Delhi.

The committee was convinced that several of these so-called

'encounters' never took place. It had received evidence from people who saw the police arresting several of those later shot in so-called 'encounters' being taken from their homes quite peaceably. Witnesses had also testified to the brutal manner in which they were tortured. The purpose of the torture seems to have been to compel them to confess to crimes in which the police were implicating them, and to have them implicate those the police had specified.

The report went on to state:

In none of these cases did the State authorities hold any inquest over the dead bodies as they are required to do under Section 174 of the Criminal Procedure Code 1973. The details of these crimes have now been sent to the Union Home Minister and copies of statements of witnesses attached to them. A request has been made to the Central Government to institute a judicial inquiry under the Commissions of Inquiry Act 1952 into all the deaths that are reported to have taken place during encounters in Andhra. The Act explicitly states that the Central Government can institute an inquiry on any of the items mentioned in the lists. There can be no doubt that the matter involved is of definite public importance. The State Government is so heavily involved in the crimes that an inquiry instituted by it cannot be impartial. Secondly, in order that the police officials whose names are being given to the Union Minister are not able to hamper the inquiry, we have requested the Central Government to ensure that they are suspended from duty till the inquiry is complete. Thirdly, we expect that if the inquiry indeed comes to the conclusion that the citizens were killed in cold blood and that the alleged encounters never took place, the officials concerned will be tried and punished for murder. Fourthly, we expect that if the murders are proven, the principle of ministerial responsibility and the principle of collective responsibility will be fully borne in mind and the bodies will not be quietly buried by compelling just a few junior police officers to own up to the blame for them. On more than one occasion the Chief Minister of Andhra, Mr Venegal Rao, has claimed that he has 'wiped out the Naxalites'. Fifthly, as it is entirely possible that the police will try to intimidate and even harm those who have given or will come to give evidence, we request the Central Government to ensure the safety of these witnesses.

The report then went on to describe how, out of these seventy-seven people, some bodies were found tied to trees, some with very clear evidence of torture, some with their hands and feet tied and some with their fingers chopped off; some still had their trouser bottoms and tops tied, and inside were found live rats and lizards. I am glad to say that the Union Home Minister did announce an official inquiry after he had read the report.

The next morning I went to see the 'flying yogi', Dhirendra Brahmachari. It was easy to see him, despite the fact that the press was after his blood and that every day a new story about him was brought to the notice of the people. The yogi agreed to have a quick word. He was wearing the traditional dhoti, and if I hadn't known that he was certainly in his late fifties or older, I would have estimated his age at about thirty-five. He burbled on about how he would be only too glad to talk about Mrs Gandhi and her son and the Nehru family, because, of course, they had been so good to him, etcetera. But, he said, he had the auditors in that day, so could I possibly call back tomorrow? Tomorrow was never to come: the auditors and the press saw to that. The yogi flew off to his ashram in Kashmir and was not seen back in Delhi.

In the magazine *The Current* for 21 May 1977 there was an article which described how the venerable yogi had flourished under the patronage of mother, son and caucus in pre-Janata days. Now the Janata Government had ordered a probe into his clandestine activities, sources of income and political connections. The paper also said that the yogi was in his seventies! It described his luxurious ashram in Kashmir, and said that a search party had found fairly sophisticated fire-arms and ammunition there. A Japanese twelve-bore semi-automatic rifle, two .22 telescopic rifles of American make and an English revolver of the latest model were among the goods recovered. The search party was stupefied by the wealth that overflowed from the yogi's forest abode.

The Current then added a bit more spice to the description of the yogi's life by talking about a Mr M. V. M. Ahuja. Apparently Mr Ahuja had told a court in Delhi that he had found his wife and the yogi in a compromising position on 12 July 1976 in the drawing-room of Mr Ahuja's house. Mr Ahuja then described another incident during his visits to the yogi's ashram where his wife was employed. Ahuja said that in September 1976, when his wife was constantly on night duty at the ashram, he went there at about 11.30 p.m. When he entered the bedroom of the Brahma-chari, he again found them in a compromising situation. Apparently the yogi pushed him out, told him to be a good boy and not come running back again, and bolted the door from the inside.

Poor yogi. It seems he didn't only occupy an influential position in the 'Bedroom Cabinet' of India's ex-Prime Minister!

3 The culprits

I desperately wanted to ask Mrs Gandhi two questions. Had she or had she not been responsible for all that had gone on? And if not, who were the real culprits? One thing is certain: too many people, on too many occasions, have said that whenever they needed a decision, Mrs Gandhi told them to go and talk to Sanjay Gandhi, or to Mr Bansi Lal or Mr R. K. Dhavan. Yet Sanjay held no position in the Government. And Mr Dhavan wasn't senior enough to have the Prime Minister refer to him for any decision. Yet, time and again, senior members of the Government were given orders by Sanjay or Mr Dhavan.

A friend who holds a fairly high position in the *Times of India* told me that the withdrawal of Mr P. N. Huksar was also due directly to Sanjay's behaviour. The story goes that Mr Huksar grew somewhat tired of senior members of the Government being treated in a disrespectful manner by this young man who himself knew very little about most things. He asked Mrs Gandhi that Sanjay should not be given so much unquestioned authority, particularly if she intended to take the politics of the country seriously. Mrs Gandhi refused to consider his request or do anything about Sanjay, and so Mr Huksar resigned.

Sanjay heard about the disagreement and decided to teach Mr Huksar a lesson. Mr Huksar's close relations were another well-known Delhi family, the Pandits, and Pandit Brothers is a famous shop in Connaught Place in Delhi. Old Mr Pandit is in his early eighties and is Mr Huksar's uncle, but had always been more like a father to him. Sanjay decided to take his revenge on this old gentleman. One afternoon a police car came to Connaught Place and parked half a block away from Pandit Brothers. Four policemen got out and went to search Pandit Brothers' premises. Eventually they found one towel out of a stock of thousands which was not marked with a price tag. For this unmarked towel, old Mr Pandit had been handcuffed and roughly marched across the shopping centre of New Delhi.

When the rest of his family heard about the outrage, one of the ladies decided to go and see Mrs Gandhi in person. After hearing the story, Mrs Gandhi apparently summoned Sanjay immediately. She was suitably horrified, and told Sanjay so. She also said, 'So, now your hand is reaching out to hurt even our own relatives, so maybe what they are saying out in the street about you is true. Release old Mr Pandit immediately.' To this Sanjay replied, 'Mummy, I have told you a thousand times not to interfere with what I am doing, but you insist.' At this point, it was said, he stamped his feet and carried on, saying, 'OK, I will release him, but when things go wrong and nobody is willing to stand beside you, don't come running to me like you did in 1975.'

Sanjay was obviously referring to the time when the Allahabad High Court judgement was announced and everyone in the Congress Party tried to persuade Mrs Gandhi to resign. Sanjay had been against it, because he knew that once she had resigned she would never be allowed back. Mrs Gandhi also realized this, particularly after the judge had said that she would not be allowed to stand in any elections for at least six years. While she was deciding her precise course of action, Sanjay had come to her rescue.

It was he, with R. K. Dhavan and Bansi Lal, who began to work to make it clear that, whatever the judge might say, for the people of India Mrs Gandhi was still their leader. They collected crowds of people to gather outside No. 1 Safdar Jung Road. They rang up various chief ministers of the states round Delhi and asked them to organize political rallies. Through these rallies, the judgement of the High Court was virtually turned into a non-event. Later, of course, Mr P. N. Huksar also did his bit when he drafted the pledge that all Cabinet and Chief Ministers were asked to sign. The pledge stated: 'Mrs Indira Gandhi continues to be the Prime

Minister. It is our firm and considered view that, for the integrity, stability and progress of this country, her dynamic leadership is indispensable.'

There was a great rush to sign the pledge, for by now everyone was sure that she wasn't going to quit. So a show of loyalty mattered. Mrs Gandhi believed from this moment on that it was Sanjay who had saved her. Everyone else had fumbled and hesitated, but he had gone right ahead with his two helpers and, step by step, had organized and prepared so that by midnight on 25 June the President signed the proclamation of a state of Emergency. And by 6 a.m. the following day, when she called a Cabinet meeting at her house, she knew that the arrests of J. P. Narayan and Morarji Desai had gone ahead according to plan.

Many people attributed Sanjay's hold over his mother to these few days when he and his friends, Bansi Lal and R. K. Dhavan, made her survival possible. I can understand it to a certain extent, but from this moment on she seems to have begun the handing over of her authority. Even so there were occasions when she would insist on her wishes being carried out, as with the incidents of the Pandit family or the Turkman Gate affair. But these occasions became less and less frequent. She seemed increasingly content to leave it all to Sanjay and his caucus.

Anyway, luckily for old Mr Pandit, Mrs Gandhi refused to budge over that issue and he was released. But from it we know that Sanjay had the power to persuade the police not only to go and search a shop but to arrest an old man. How the power came to him, who gave it to him, are the questions that need to be asked.

It was time for me to go back to Mrs Gandhi to see if she had made up her mind about the interviews. I found in her a marked difference. She seemed a lot more confident and relaxed, and to a certain extent unafraid. The newspapers had started reporting that she had begun to attend some functions again, particularly purely social ones organized by foreign embassies. And, even more important, she had once more begun to manipulate the Congress Party. Despite the fact that Bansi Lal had been expelled by then, she had managed to rally quite a bit of support for herself within the party.

All this was obviously helping her towards believing that

everything was not yet over. She suggested to me that a way had to be found by which she could control what I wrote more closely. I pointed out that the book would be valid only if it remained independent and unbiased.

She understood this, but said, 'My experience of journalists is not really a happy one, and if I agree to this, it has to be left entirely under my control. Your loyalty to your publisher might make it impossible.'

'Are you trying to tell me that such a book must be commissioned by you?' I asked.

'Yes,' she said, 'that would be a way out. In fact it is the only way out.'

'But that will not do any good, because it will be like so many other things written about you. People will not believe any of it, because I would have worked for you and been paid by you.'

I tried to reason, but she was adamant. She felt that too many people had promised her one thing and done another. I had no alternative now but to opt out since I knew that the only book that could have any kind of merit would be one written independently. As I progressed in my research, and new inquiries about Sanjay continued to be announced together with hints about possible inquiries into Mrs Gandhi as well, I realized why she could not allow anyone to talk to her in depth. She was too vulnerable. Ironically, because of this fact, a sympathetic but independent assessment could have done her a lot of good. But she couldn't see it – or not at this moment, anyway.

At one point Mr P. N. Huksar said to me that I shouldn't blame either Sanjay or Mrs Gandhi too easily. After all, he was a mere boy and she had had a difficult life – a life of great loneliness which had left her incapable of any close relationship. She had surrounded herself with people out to get what they could from her, including her son Sanjay, and it was clear to see that she had some kind of guilt complex about her children.

The reason may be that she had treated them much as her father had treated her. He had never been there. He had been involved in the national freedom movement. He had been in jail so much of the time that the only real contact he had with his daughter had often been through the letters he wrote to her from prison. As she is reported to have said once, 'My father loved me a lot, but only through letters. He was never there himself, not when my mother was ill, or when I needed him.' The irony of fate is that she did the same to her two boys. They were sent to a boarding school, and she became a mother through letters alone, and had, one suspects, been compensating her children for their deprivation ever since.

The reason why Mrs Gandhi lost the election in the end was, I think, because she had isolated herself so much from the reality of India that she had no idea how unpopular she had become. Bansi Lal, Sanjay and R. K. Dhavan had all been against holding elections, perhaps because they feared the results of the excesses they had practised. On the other hand, they had regularly from time to time organized rallies in her support to quieten any doubts she may have felt. What she didn't realize was that the crowds outside her house and in the rallies had been paid to come, and were actually brought there in hired public buses. Had she known that, maybe she would never have announced the elections. And had the caucus anticipated that their planned persuasion of her popularity would be their undoing, they would surely have let some truth filter through. But perhaps they were afraid that if she knew the extent to which people were resentful, then she might have put her foot down, if only as a reflex from her democratic upbringing. This the caucus obviously could not afford. Such questions will doubtless remain unanswered as only Mrs Gandhi herself would be able to answer them and there seems little chance of her doing so.

Meanwhile I needed to know whether there were indeed going to be any official inquiries about her, so I asked among several government officials. The answer from each of them was the same: 'Love to have a go, but there aren't any witnesses left.'

I didn't understand. 'What do you mean, no witnesses left?'

'Just that. They have died or mysteriously disappeared. So there are no key witnesses at all. The only remaining ones are those who themselves were accomplices of the ex-Prime Minister, Mrs Gandhi. In some cases even people around the witnesses have conveniently disappeared.'

When Mrs Gandhi was interviewed by David Frost recently on British television I happened to be watching. It was an incredible performance because she still continued to claim that Sanjay had had no authority, that the excesses during the Emergency had happened only because of a few over-enthusiastic officers. Mr Frost must have been unaware of the incidents in which Sanjay was directly implicated or I am sure that he would have tried to pin-point her. Here are some of the questions she should have been asked:

1. Why, and with what authority, did Sanjay Gandhi stand and give the orders for the shanty town outside Turkman Gate to be bulldozed? It is reported that Mrs Gandhi rushed to the scene as soon as she heard and tried to stop the whole operation. She succeeded, but she must have known and seen Sanjay there. Why did she not tell him then that he simply did not have the authority to give such orders?
2. Why did she not stop the Chief Ministers of various states from bowing down to Sanjay? According to Mrs Ambika Soni, the then President of the Youth Congress, whenever Sanjay visited any state, Chief Ministers would receive him as though he was the head of Government. The facts were widely reported in the press. I know that Mrs Gandhi did ask the Chief Ministers not to go and receive Sanjay, but also that when they continued to do so, she did nothing more about it.
3. Why was it impossible for any senior minister or senior government official to go directly to the Prime Minister? Why should they have to have gone either via Sanjay or Bansi Lal or R. K. Dhavan? If a team of cabinet ministers and officials did not have direct access to the Prime Minister, then something was clearly wrong in the system somewhere and needed to be rectified.
4. What of the several jewellers around India who openly talk about the time when Sanjay Gandhi and his wife came to political rallies and selected jewellery worth anything from 50,000 to 150,000 rupees? Then went away with the jewellery without paying the price? In fact, one jeweller in Gwalior asked for his money, and for his nerve had his elder brother put in jail. If my son suddenly turned up with even one large diamond, I would like to know where he got it. Why did Mrs Gandhi never question Sanjay?

Many unsavoury stories about Sanjay Gandhi and women were also in circulation. It was alleged that there had been rapes, fathers who committed suicide, daughters who committed suicide, and so on and so forth. It was said that the daughter of Mr Mohan Meakin of Meakin Breweries was one such victim and that Mr Meakin never recovered from the shock of Sanjay not marrying his daughter. The story also went that even Sanjay's eventual marriage had only taken place because his wife Monica's father had pulled a gun. Monica's father has since died. His body was found in a field near Delhi. He had been shot through the head. A verdict of suicide was given, though no gun was found beside the body. But apparently he had been depressed about the various impending inquiries into Sanjay's Maruti Empire.

The newspapers reported Sanjay's escapades with girls over several years. Is it really possible that Mrs Gandhi knew nothing of his reputation? I can accept that there was maybe some exaggeration in the stories. But let us not forget that Mr Sagar Suri, a personal friend of Sanjay's, had given him an apartment in his well-known apartment block in Delhi. Furthermore, he had also allowed the *Times of India* to rent an apartment close to Sanjay's. Thus the visiting journalists were able to keep a fairly close watch on who came and went at Sanjay's flat, and according to them the truth was not far behind the rumours. The fact remains that I was able to discover all these rumours and news items as well as eye-witnesses to various incidents very easily during a period of seven weeks, and I don't live in India. So how can Mrs Gandhi have known nothing? And if she did know, why did she do nothing to restrain Sanjay?

It seems to me that the answer to all such questions can only be a simple one: she had become completely dependent on Sanjay and his caucus. It took a little time, but as the months of the Emergency passed, so she questioned them less and less and listened to outsiders only on increasingly rare occasions.

When I interviewed Ambika Soni, the President of the Youth Congress during the Emergency and a close friend of both Sanjay and Mrs Gandhi, she said something interesting. I asked her if she herself had noticed any change in Mrs Gandhi. 'Yes,' she said. 'The change was a slow one. In the beginning Mrs Gandhi listened to everything with an open mind, and thought about it, and talked about it, and if she agreed would do something about it. Then she began to listen but not do anything. And in the last few months she didn't even want to hear anything. So the change was definitely there, and I am not sure that it was for the better.'

Many others have said much the same thing. Ambika Soni still states that the only reason she joined the Congress Party was because of Mrs Gandhi, and that when she first met Mrs Gandhi she found her a strong and progressive leader. She was also struck by the fact that Mrs Gandhi paid attention to anybody who had something to say, however junior they were. And this fact was reflected in the character of Mrs Gandhi's earlier days as Prime Minister.

At the beginning she did indeed surround herself with brilliant minds, whose advice she took seriously. Her associates included men of the old Indian civil service or of the Indian administrative service. She had among her advisers Mr P. N. Huksar, Mr Dhar and Mr Sharada Prasad. There was a lot of goodwill in the country for it looked as though at last progress was possible. Many constructive things happened. She manoeuvred her party well and in 1969 got rid of those she regarded as reactionaries. She came through the Bangladesh crises and showed much courage, and people were full of admiration for her.

But then things seemed to start to go wrong. Even natural calamities helped her towards the road on which she eventually found herself. India had three successive droughts, and the unemployment figures soared. Because of this student unrest began, and every day there were strikes. All the ills that had remained under the surface became apparent. Communal riots occurred and every day there would be a protest march of some sort through the streets. Every day there would be hunger strikes outside ministers' residences. Then some of the labour strikes began to get out of hand. An inquiry was begun into Maruti Limited. Mrs Gandhi must have slowly begun to feel hemmed in. And maybe she also began to feel that her brilliant advisers were not really succeeding in getting India anywhere. And so began the slow but deadly process of her turning away from all the worthwhile people who were ready to help her and the turning more and more towards those who produced quick results and used unscrupulous means. The more insecure she felt, the more prone to flattery she became. Eventually all those with scruples had left her and the stage was set for what followed.

It is said that the system as it evolved during the last four years of Mrs Gandhi's rule bred sycophancy. There was such fear among those who surrounded her that there was no longer any way she could have learnt the truth. But this in itself represents an unforgivable sin on the part of the prime minister of a country. If a prime minister alienates the system by misusing it to the extent where the system cannot respond or function, then he or she has failed in their duty. No one is exempt from learning to use the system.

First of all, if you sit in the highest office of the land you cannot afford to have favourites. If you do have them, you certainly must never make the knowledge public. If you do fail in both these things, then you must at all costs avoid granting uncalled-for or premature promotions for your favourites. It seems to me that by her failure to operate the system, Mrs Gandhi laid herself open to being surrounded by such devious people that her downfall was inevitable.

I have heard that Mr Bansi Lal and others have begged the people to forgive them for their mistakes and blunders, but that the people threw shoes, eggs and tomatoes in reply. And when Bansi Lal's own sister stood against him in the General Election, she won. The people of India have not forgiven the caucus, and it remains a difficult thing to forgive. The list of horrors continues to grow.

Take the inquiry into the death of a so-called dacoit or bandit, called Sundar. Sundar died while in police custody. How he managed it is not known, but his death was due to drowning. But before he became a 'bandit' Sundar had apparently had a very beautiful sister who came to the attention of Sanjay Gandhi. As the story goes, Sanjay slept with the girl, who then found that she was pregnant and killed herself. Sanjay, true to form, tried to wash his hands of the whole affair, but Sundar became a dacoit and swore that he would kill Sanjay. So a massive manhunt was started. In due course Sundar was captured, but later the poor man drowned, mysteriously and in unknown circumstances, while in his prison cell.

A long time ago, during the British Raj, when Maharaj Nand Kumar was charged with high treason and hanged, many stories went around, for Nand Kumar was the first Brahmin ever to be hanged in India. I once read a record of his trial when I was going through a very patriotic phase in my early teens. The trial was interesting since it was obvious from the start that the man had been framed. During the time when the most vital eye-witness was giving his evidence, a supporter of Nand Kumar raised one finger to him, but the witness shook his head. The man then raised two fingers, and the witness still shook his head. Eventually the man raised five fingers, and the witness nodded. The five fingers had meant 500,000 rupees, and the witness was willing at that price. He ended his testimony at that point by saying, 'And then, my Lord, I woke up and realized that all that I had thought that I had seen had in fact been a dream.' There was, of course, uproar in the court, and everybody thought that now the case would be dismissed. But no such luck. This was the hey-day of the British Raj. The judge announced in a ringing pompous voice that, 'India is such a hot country that it is very difficult to assess when one is awake and when one is asleep and dreaming.' And he sentenced Maharaj Nand Kumar to death by hanging.

This was a story that we were all told in our childhood, and it filled us all with indignation, it was so humiliating. But, we told ourselves, this had only been possible because this was a British government and it didn't give a damn about our country.

After India became independent, the judiciary of India was one thing that we were all quite proud of. The courts remained painfully slow and very expensive, but if you were genuinely innocent and didn't care how long it took to prove your innocence, then you could be fairly certain of winning your case.

A colleague of my father was wrongfully dismissed from his job. His senior officer had had a row with him and found an excuse to sack him. So he sued the Government of India. It took him nearly two years, but in the end he won his case. In the process his family suffered, since all their savings went into lawyers' fees, but win he did. He then got his job back, with all the salary due to him and no loss of seniority. My father used to laugh and say with great pride that this was the only country in the world where the Government frequently lost a case. Somehow it maintained our faith in democracy.

But how is an Indian to console himself when he discovers acts of corruption in an Indian Court when the Government is entirely Indian? And, as if to crown it all, when that same Government is headed by Nehru's daughter – that same Nehru whom we called 'The Uncrowned Prince of India', the adopted and chosen King of all the Indians.

There is a flaw in Mrs Gandhi's argument when she says that

certain over-zealous officers were responsible for certain atrocities, or that she can't personally be held responsible for the corruption of her officers. The fact remains that if the officer in charge is honest, then those working under him are likely to remain comparatively honest also. But men working under a dishonest officer will soon learn to copy and go further; and, moreover, the officer is not himself then in a position to stop them since his own slate is far from clean.

Youth Congress members were accused of collecting vast sums of money in the name of Sanjay Gandhi. When I interviewed Mrs Ambika Soni, the President of the Youth Congress, she said again and again that she had tried to tell people to come forward with the names of those going about collecting money in the name of Sanjay Gandhi and the Youth Congress, but nobody had come forward. No doubt they had been afraid to do so. But somebody somewhere must at some point have begun collecting money from the people in the name of Sanjay Gandhi and the Youth Congress with Sanjay's full knowledge. What followed can only happen once this sort of thing becomes accepted behaviour. Ambika Soni threw some light on some other interesting areas. She claimed that she herself had repeatedly tried to warn Mrs Gandhi about what people were saying about Rukhsana Sultana and Sanjay, but that Mrs Gandhi chose to take no notice on the first occasion, and on the second told Ambika to go and see Sanjay. Sanjay dismissed Ambika with the remark that, 'Rukhsana does not need Youth Congress, Youth Congress needs Rukhsana.' Ambika tried to tell him that Rukhsana was possibly using the Youth Congress's name for not very legitimate goings on, and was thus giving a bad name to everybody concerned. But Sanjay airily dismissed the whole thing.

According to Ambika, she tried on one last occasion to warn Mrs Gandhi about Rukhsana, but when she arrived saw that Mrs Gandhi was greeting some dignitaries with Rukhsana at her side. At point she decided it was perhaps all too late and left. Later she clashed with Mr Bansi Lal, the disagreement resulting in her not being given a ticket for the General Elections. When she appealed to Sanjay about Bansi Lal and his methods, Sanjay had just said, 'I trust Mr Bansi Lal so much that I will go blindfold wherever he leads me.'

He still goes about saying similar things. I wonder if he realizes where he has actually been led. Ambika Soni also claims that she tried to protest about the undesirable elements who were suddenly being recruited into the Youth Congress, but to no avail. It seems that the young bullies, delinquents and good-for-nothings who got into the Youth Congress, collected by fair means or foul a lot of money for Sanjay, had a good time in the process and caused a lot of people a lot of suffering; and eventually became a major reason for the downfall of Congress in the elections.

It has been alleged that Ambika was Sanjay's mistress until Rukhsana Sultana came on the scene. It is also known that Ambika was a very influential lady while she was in favour. The Youth Congress's funds were vast, and it is known that they were misappropriated. Several people from the caucus have recently been arrested for syphoning £4 million out of Youth Congress funds into private non-existent companies. How much was Ambika aware of this? Is it possible that she says all these things now to keep clear of the mess? But the main point in her favour remains that she was refused a ticket in the last General Elections, and that it is known that it was on Mr Bansi Lal's insistence that she was refused the ticket. Had she been a part of the caucus till the end, she would have been given her ticket.

There is one other interesting aspect of Ambika's story. Towards the end of the Emergency, she said, she began to raise her voice more and more against the new unruly elements in the Youth Congress. In the end, Mr Bansi Lal grew angry and began to tell Mrs Gandhi that Sanjay should be made the President of the Youth Congress. Ambika was asked to resign. After some argument she realized that she was on a losing wicket and agreed to do so. A date was fixed for Sanjay's takeover. The night before the takeover, Mrs Gandhi checked with Ambika, and all was going ahead as planned. But early on the next morning, at about 7 a.m., Ambika had a telephone call in which Mrs Gandhi stated that under no circumstances must Sanjay become President of the Youth Congress. Ambika promised and withdrew her resignation.

Ambika can offer no explanation as to why this happened. And I have wondered if the rumours I had heard were correct. It was being said that the caucus around Mrs Gandhi wanted Sanjay to be the power, because only with him in the driving seat could they themselves exercise real power. Mrs Gandhi had a habit of putting her foot down every now and again. Because of this, it was said, even her life might be in danger, for these really were unscrupulous men who wouldn't allow anyone to stand in their way. So maybe – just maybe – she had an inkling of this, and that was why she put a stop to Sanjay being made President of the Youth Congress. Whatever the reasons, Ambika was willing to let me record this interview and to quote her wherever necessary. She said that she was not ashamed of saying openly and happily that she only became involved in politics because of Mrs Gandhi. She said that she had believed that Mrs Gandhi could make an excellent leader of this country. She had had the guts and the ability until the change happened. And after that there was no getting through to her.

This is the story as it is told by almost everybody who was closely involved with Mrs Gandhi. Subhadra Joshi, who was a Congress party worker for years and an MP from Delhi, published a long tale of woe while I was in India. She said the same things: that she had gone to warn Mrs Gandhi about Rukhsana's evil influence on the voters, and how Sanjay's 'Clean Delhi Campaign' was certainly going to lose her the elections.

Subhadra Joshi evidently also tried to have something done about the Turkman Gate affair, but to no avail. The same sort of attempts were made by her to talk to Mrs Gandhi about the vasectomy drives, but nobody listened or paid attention.

Now Subhadra Joshi may not be the most dynamic of person-alities, but there is one undisputed fact about her: she is an absolutely, totally reliable and trustworthy worker of the Congress Party. From her testimony it became clear that even old and steady workers who were really the party's foundation were ignored by Mrs Gandhi and her favourites.

It's sad to see how the Congress Party has changed over the years. When India first became independent, it was full of idealists, visionaries, people who really cared about India. Then Gandhi died, and the Congress Party did not, as he had asked, dissolve itself. These were tired old men, who had fought long for the freedom of India, and it must have been difficult for them to give it all up and go to some small village to start a social revolu-tion. A few left and began field work. A few others became more disillusioned and left politics altogether. And a few became passionately involved in their careers. But the backbone of the party remained undamaged. It was full of such grand old men as

Govind Vallabh Panth, Kidwai, Rajagopalachari, Sardar Patel and Bal Krishna Sharma 'Navin', to name but a few.

Nevertheless, the change was happening, and in a way it was inevitable, however heartbreaking. I remember once asking why the change was happening. The question was put to an old friend of my father's, Mahavir Tyagi, a much respected member of parliament. I remember his answer with great clarity. 'We were blessed with a philosopher's stone in Gandhi,' he said. 'Whatever Gandhi touched became gold. Now he is dead and we are back to being the cheap metal we always were.'

I think he was being a little harsh, because I don't think that they had all changed as quickly as all that. But ambitions were taking hold, comforts were becoming important. Politics is a strange beast, and it always ends up by consuming its adherents. It was no different in India with the Congress Party. The intrigues began and slowly grew worse. Groups were formed within the party which manoeuvred each other's candidates into or out of power. Some groups split away and joined the opposition benches. A lot of criticism was levelled against the industrialization of India, which Nehru had so passionately set about achieving, for this went absolutely against the Gandhian philosophy on which the Congress Party was based.

What did not, however, change and was only strengthened were the democratic principles. People could oppose Nehru and the ruling party and nothing terrible happened to them. There were disappointments and problems, but India was surviving them and so was the Congress Party. There was Kashmir, which to this day remains a problem, there were the Naga Land problems in the north, and later, of course, the Chinese invasion. But despite all this, there was an air of hope and excitement, and compared to recent years, Congress played a clean game.

Then Nehru died. Suddenly things began to look shaky. Mr Lal Bahadur Shastri took over and was much loved by the Indians but he didn't last long under the pressures. He died of a heart attack within a few months of taking over. In all this time the Congress Party had remained the ruling party, and the opposition was split into so many small groups that it looked like always remaining in power. Mrs Gandhi had begun to come into the limelight during Mr Shastri's time, and now the real intrigues began and Mr Kamraj brought Mrs Gandhi right into the front line. She became, to start with, a stop-gap Prime Minister. From this point onwards, the Congress Party began to change its character. It was all moves of chess and who was backing whom and what were the strengths behind them which became the order of the day.

Mrs Gandhi strengthened herself and, despite the fact that Mr Morarji Desai and Jag-Jivan Ram both wanted to become Prime Minister, she stayed in power. Within the party began the move to try to get rid of all that was reactionary or old-fashioned. It was said that Congress needed a face-lift and that Mrs Gandhi was the person to provide it. This was the golden era of Mrs Gandhi but perhaps the opposite for the party itself. In 1969 Mrs Gandhi managed to split the party and a lot of the old-timers left or were forced to leave. It was called a mini revolution. But I think what it did achieve was that from that moment onwards the Congress Party – the new one that is – began to use for survival the weapon of flattery. It became less important to say and know what was good for the party, and more important to please the Boss, because you couldn't survive if you didn't do that. They had seen it happen to old hands like Morarji Desai and they were determined that the same fate would not befall them.

Then came the Bangladesh crisis, and on the surface things looked good for Mrs Gandhi and her new Congress Party. But the inside was being eaten away with this disease, and as the national crises began to pile up – food crisis, unemployment, labour disputes, corruption, student agitations – the party just eroded.

When the Emergency was declared in June 1975 there really wasn't even a peep out of her ministers and her chief ministers. In fact a lot of them were kept in the dark about it until the President had signed the proclamation.

It is possible that all this was inevitable because the Congress Party had been in power for too long. It is also possible that Mahatma Gandhi was right and that a new party should have been created at the time of Independence whose aims were to do with developing a nation. These are unanswerable questions. What is certain is that the caucus around Mrs Gandhi created and kept a bunch of gutless men whom they called the Congress Party. These people still do not have the courage to stand up and say, let the purge of the party begin. Immediately after the sweeping victory of the Janata Party, Congress Party's President was elected. And despite a lot of noise, Mrs Gandhi still managed to have her man elected as the President, Mr Brahmananda Reddy.

Soon after I began to write this book a number of people were arrested. All of them were allowed bail, and the charges made public were only two. First, the misappropriation of party funds and syphoning them off into non-existent private companies, the amounts quoted being £6 million of Congress Party funds and £4 million of Youth Congress funds. Secondly, gross misuse of authority. The names of those arrested are as follows:

1. Bansi Lal – ex-Defence Minister
2. Y. P. Kapoor – PA to Mrs Gandhi
3. R. K. Dhavan – PA to Mrs Gandhi
4. V. C. Shukla – ex-Minister of Information and Broadcasting
5. K. D. Maliya
6. P. C. Sethi
7. N. K. Singh
8. H. R. Gokhle
9. D. P. Chattoperdhyaya
10. B. B. Vohra
11. R. N. Aggarwal
12. N. V. Arunachalam
13. K. K. Birla

All of these were close associates or on the personal staff of Mrs Gandhi and Sanjay.

Whatever the outcome of the witch-hunt, and however many of those who were at the top are arrested and punished, it will not be enough. Because it is not only those who carried out orders who are guilty. The ones who kept silent because it was easier or because it saved a few privileges are equally guilty. And I hope that the shame of this realization remains with us for ever, for it might help to make India a cleaner place in which to live in the future.

4 The aftermath

The key date was 18 January 1977. This was the day when Mrs Gandhi announced that she had decided to dissolve the Lok Sabha, the Indian Lower House, and to hold fresh elections. It took the world by storm and Indians refused to believe it. But, true to her word, Mrs Gandhi relaxed the Emergency and released the political prisoners so that they could prepare their election campaign. It is still a mystery as to why she announced the election. So far as I know, everyone close to her was against it. But she was adamant. Evidently she really did believe the reports which her intelligence people kept sending her. Mr P. N. Huksar has said that he thinks it was a straight political gamble. Mrs Gandhi felt that if she went to the Indian people, reminded them of all the good she had done in the past and asked for their forgiveness, then she would get it.

And nobody else really believed that she would lose. As the campaign progressed, everyone thought it would be neck-and-neck all the way, but that in the end Congress would creep in with a tiny majority. In fact the fear that the Congress Party would be returned was very great in the people's hearts, as was illustrated by the confession that a journalist friend made to me. The first Janata Party rally, he said, which took place in Karolbagh in Delhi, had not been covered by any newspaper reporter. The press had relied on what the Samachar Agency – a creation of Mrs Gandhi – reported. But as the reports came in, and it became clear that well over a million people had attended that rally, they began to realize that the tide could well be turning. Even then, when the second rally took place in the same Ram Lila grounds where Mrs Gandhi had announced the Emergency in June 1975, journalists were still reluctant to go themselves to cover it. In the end it was decided that about ten or twelve of them would get in one large car and cruise the area, and only if it all looked worthwhile would they stop and listen. When they got there they discovered that the crowds were several million. And that despite the size of the crowds, it was a well-ordered assembly. It was then that the journalists got out and decided that if all these millions of people had the guts to say openly that they wanted to hear the leaders of the Janata Party, then it was time that they should join them.

The election campaign on each side was a revelation in itself. The Congress Party and Mrs Gandhi had vast resources at their disposal: jeeps, helicopters and trucks to take them from one place to the other. The Janata Party, on the other hand, had nothing. Or nothing but enormous numbers of student volunteers and individuals willing to give time, money and other resources to back the Janata Party. As the excitement rose, the Congress Party began to get more and more nervous. It was becoming obvious that people no longer wanted to hear what the Congress candidates had to say. Janata Party rallies were the only ones to draw a massed.crowd.

On 2 February 1977 the bottom fell out of the Congress Party's election plans. Mr Jag-Jivan Ram decided to resign from the party and the Government. Nobody had expected this to happen. and now the tide really did turn. And for the first time Mrs Gandhi began to show alarm. But by now it was already too late. The machinery for the elections had been set in motion and there was no way anyone could stop it.

Mrs Gandhi experienced heckling in her rallies. She was told point-blank by people that she should get rid of Sanjay. Sanjay himself had unpleasant experiences in Umethi, his own con- stituency. His constituents not only did not want to hear him, but expressed their dislike openly. No amount of money spent by Congress managed to switch the direction of events. In certain areas, the Congress candidates were giving away not only money but stainless-steel pots and pans. And people took all the gifts,

71

thanked the candidates profusely and said they were still going to vote for the Janata Party. The masses of India had decided to get rid of what they considered to be evil. The Janata Party came in with a sweeping majority at the elections.

There was jubilant dancing in the streets and crowds of people waited outside newspaper offices and roared approval as each Janata Party victory was pinned on the board. Outside the *Times of India* offices the little man pinning the results on the boards was actually showered with money since he was giving the people the good news they had been waiting for.

Mrs Gandhi returned to Delhi on 18 March. By that time most of the polling was over and the situation looked ominous for the Congress Party. Meetings held at the Prime Minister's residence were attended by Sanjay, R. K. Dhavan, Bansi Lal and Om Mehta. It was rumoured that if the elections went against her she would declare martial law. The Law Ministry experts thought that it was possible to impose martial law without the army being called in. In which case, she would have called on the Border Security Forces. But thankfully this remained only a rumour, and in the event Mrs Gandhi gracefully resigned.

In the end, of course, she had no other choice after she herself lost her seat in Rai Bareli to her age-old rival, Mr Raj Narain, the man who began it all by bringing a court case against her in 1971. People were as shocked by the news as she was herself. The shock lasted quite a few days, for when I met her about three weeks after the results it was clear that she still hadn't recovered. Mrs Gandhi had been afraid that people would come to attack her house or do her harm. But none of this took place. People felt almost sorry for her. The one person for whom there was no word of kindness was Sanjay.

The euphoria of the elections lasted a few days as people began to talk and laugh loudly in the streets. Then, with equal enthusiasm, everything in the administration began to be put back as it had been before the Emergency. One or two brave little mud huts appeared overnight in a patch that had been cleared by Sanjay. A hunger striker appeared in a street in the heart of New Delhi. The prices began to creep up bit by bit. On the political scene, the Janata Party began to settle in and try and get on with the task of forming a government. People had begun to do all the things that they had been unable to do during the past twenty months. There was an outburst of petty crime everywhere. There were repeated demands from various unions for strike action. Students, not wanting to be left behind, began their usual protest marches and strikes. Amazingly, as though by magic, the black market re-opened. Things that disappeared from the shop windows were of course available at a higher price from the back door. 'Black' money also began to appear in the business world. Films that had been pending because of its scarcity for the last two years suddenly began to be made.

While all this was happening, people kept saying that now there is no Emergency, no Sanjay and no Mrs Gandhi, our problems are over. It struck me that the people of India really believed that whatever they did now wouldn't matter because the Janata Party would solve everything. As I realized, a lot of this was due to the fact that they had been unable to protest about anything for nearly two years. The pent-up energy needed release. But as time went on I could still see no signs from Janata Party Ministers which were likely to stop the destructive outbursts. I decided I needed to know a little more about this Janata Party, so I arranged for myself to be invited to the first Janata Party Conference in Delhi. It turned out to be a devastating experience.

The conference was held in the permanent exhibition building in the middle of New Delhi, and my memory of it begins with the enormous echoing dome. Rickety old school chairs were provided for the press, while the rest of the hall floor was covered with rugs on which representatives sat. Facing us was an enormous stage. At the back of the stage was a garlanded photograph of Jai Prakash Narayan. There were thousands of people. The area where they were supposed to sit was not really large enough, and so in the middle of the clapping and chaos fights kept breaking out. Someone would have taken someone else's place, or somebody had stepped on somebody's toes, or somebody was sitting in the wrong area – there were so many fights that I am sure they were fighting about anything under the sun.

It seemed incredible that those sitting on the stage made no attempt to quieten the people or stop the disturbances. They went on speaking as though making a speech was the one thing that mattered. It looked comical, almost like a montage from a film. The various activities inside the dome appeared not to be connected with each other. There were the people who were fighting, and those who were applauding, there were those who were speaking and those who were making notes – and nobody had anything to do with anyone else.

On the stage I could see Morarji Desai, Acharya Kriplani, Mrs Vijay Lakshmi Pandit, Raj Narain, Charan Singh and other old-timers. Mr Jag-Jivan Ram had not yet joined them, but no doubt this would happen fairly soon. At the back I could see George Fernandes, Chandra Shekhar, Madhu Dandvate, L. K. Advani, Bahuguna and others. I looked at the front row of these tired old men and felt a sense of shock. They seemed no more than showmen, looking only for applause. In order to get it, they would raise their hands and make speeches, smile and wave to the crowds, always trying to get a little louder applause than the fellow before. Tired, ambitious old men, making their last bid for power. And around them the crowd sat riveted and waiting for the miracle. Every now and then a lull in the fights still going on around us allowed us actually to hear what was being said.

Those that were sitting had their eyes fixed on the stage – their faces so full of desperation and their desire to will something to happen being so strong and so real that I could feel it throbbing under my feet. Their expectations seemed to be saying to them: now we are suddenly free from corruption, free from oppression, there will be employment for everybody, food for everybody, and the legendary Utopia which the Ramayana talks about in terms of 'Ram Rajya' will arrive at any minute and stay for ever. The people were waiting for this miracle from their leaders, but all I could see were blind ageing men with infirm hands and legs in command of a huge rickety ship. And all around the poor ship a storm was raging.

It struck me that none of these men had the strength or the ability to be the masters of the ship they had inherited. Their driving force was not love for their country but personal ambition. Their faces lit up only with single-minded selfishness. Their eyes were filled not with the dreams and visions of my country but with greed. Their eyes indeed lacked the lustre, clarity and perception required to share the dreams of their fellow men. They were pale, yellowing, short-sighted eyes, which could only see as far as their own families' interests. Looking at them, I feared for the noble and quixotic J. P. Narayan, whose name they used so freely. They needed him at that moment for their ambition, but what would happen once their ambition had been fulfilled I dreaded to think. God forgive us, I thought, the driving force of our leaders seems not to be God, religion, society or country, or any of the things which might give India a ray of hope for the future. Ambition seemed such a petty motive that my heart trembled for the land of my forefathers.

I sat through the three hours or so of the conference, and the only time when I breathed easily was when some of the newer and younger members of the Cabinet spoke. Where the old talked not from their souls but with a calculated effect to get the loudest applause, the younger ones seemed far more matter-of-fact.

After the conference we sat in the hotel coffee lounge and I poured my heart out to a journalist friend, Mr J. D. Singh, who had taken me there. My doubts, fears and hopes all came tumbling out. He listened gravely and with concern, and then said, 'Why don't you go and see some of these people that are worrying you so much?'

Why not, indeed? Such a simple solution. So I arranged to meet Mr Jag-Jivan Ram, now our Defence Minister, Mr Bahuguna, our Petroleum Minister, and Mr Charan Singh, our Home Affairs Minister.

All three of them are senior, respected politicians in India. They have been involved in the Indian Government in one capacity or the other for very many years. Mr Bahuguna, the youngest of the three, has ambitions of one day being Prime Minister, and it was easy enough to get hold of him in the first instance. I saw him, explained about the book, told him that I wanted the answer to only one question. He had himself been a part of the Government of Mrs Gandhi, but had been unable to stop the Emergency or any of the atrocities. What made him think that the story was going to be different this time?

Perhaps he was a trifle offended, but I explained that this really was the only question that would make sense and be reassuring to the people of India. I also said that I intended to put the self-same question, among others, to all the older members that I could contact in the Cabinet.

He grinned then and said, 'OK, but I would like to have the question written down and think about it a little before answering, so why don't you come back in a couple of days' time.'

This seemed fair enough, so I thanked him, came out, saw his

PA and fixed another appointment. The story was much the same in each of the three gentlemen's offices, so I typed out my question, took it back to the offices, fixed another appointment and waited.

Mr Bahuguna in fact saw me on two further occasions, but each time declined to let me record his answer, saying, 'We really need more time to sit down and talk.' Eventually he got involved in the State Elections and I had to return to England.

Mr Charan Singh, the Home Affairs Minister, I never got to see. His PAs changed with remarkable rapidity. The person I spoke to on the telephone was never the one whom I saw in the office and never the one that I gave my questions to. After having delivered questions to three different people, seen three totally different men and spoken to three other men I just gave up with Mr Charan Singh. It was obvious that his various PAs never communicated with each other, and that there was no system by which one could leave messages.

This left Mr Jag-Jivan Ram, our Defence Minister and the man supposed to have been responsible for turning the tide against Mrs Gandi. It is generally believed that it was when Mr Ram decided to ditch Mrs Gandhi that victory for the Janata Party became a certainty. Mr Ram has a reputation for being a shrewd politician, and one whose sense of timing would leave many a great actor gasping with envy. I saw him at his home one evening.

The place was packed with ordinary people clutching files in their hands and hoping that the great man would solve their problem. Second-rate politicians from the provinces had high hopes of getting the old man to give them his blessing so that they too could bask in his sunshine. I was kept waiting for about twenty minutes and then shown into his office. Spotlessly white handwoven cotton dhoti; a white kurta and a white cap; bushy eyebrows, silver hair, clumps of black hair sticking out of his ears; a beaming smile – that is my memory of Mr Ram. As I explained what I hoped to do, he kept smiling as though the smile had been stuck on his face in perpetuity. I worried for a moment or two whether he could actually hear me. My doubts turned out to be without foundation, because as soon as I finished he said, the smile still pasted on his face, 'Bring the questions to my PA and I will see them.'

'Will you then let me record an interview?'

'Yes, of course. I will tell the PA to look at the questions carefully and draft the answers. I will then read them out and you can record.'

I was speechless . . . A PA to draft the answers! I eventually found my voice and, seething with anger and trying hard not to show it, said, 'I wanted your answers, not those of a PA. You sit in this chair, not your PA.'

A veil came over the eyes, the smile remained pasted, and with great patience he said, as if talking to a slow-witted child, 'It's all right, the PA knows what I think and would like to say.'

Struggling to keep my temper I got up, thanked him abruptly and walked out. I never went back to Mr Ram.

I felt that my despair in the Janata Party Conference had been well founded. These people had not changed, and there was no way for them to change, and really everything hinged on whether they died before their attitudes infected the new generation of politicians. I found myself involuntarily hoping and praying that this would happen.

Then I thought that maybe I ought to see Mr Desai, the new Prime Minister of India. As it happened, an old acquaintance of my father's was working in the Prime Minister's office and I went to see him to find out if there was any possibility of my being able to interview the Prime Minister. Two visits to the Prime Minister's office convinced me that there was little point in trying to talk to him. As I soon discovered, a biography of him had already been commissioned by the Government and its title was to be, *The Saint Prime Minister of India*. (I hope they change it before publication!) So my general impression was that everything was much the same. Flattery remained the shortest route to recognition.

I did actually get to see Mr Desai briefly, but he himself said that he didn't really see any point in my interviewing him, because he couldn't really answer any questions as it was too soon. But he did give his blessings to the book. He is physically a very impressive man, much younger looking than his eighty-two years. He is known as a man of principles. He is a strict vegetarian. He does not smoke or drink. He now eats no cooked food at all, but only fruit and milk. He is strong-willed and ambitious, and he does have a habit of referring to God too many times in his conversation. This worried me, because it made him sound like one of those men who never do or say anything without a direct order from God. He had clashed swords with Mrs Gandhi many times in the past. But this time, of course, he had won.

During my visits to the Prime Minister's office I discovered that his closest personal adviser is Mr Shankar. Now Mr Shankar is an interesting figure, for ever since I can remember he had been a 'Birla man'. Being a 'Birla man' means that Mr Shankar had been employed by one of the leading Indian industrialists, Mr G. D. Birla. Mr Morarji Desai had personally asked for Mr Shankar to be brought out of retirement.

Mr Birla held an influence over the Congress Government in some way or another ever since India became free. That was one weakness which Mahatma Gandhi introduced into India's politics for which I find it difficult to forgive him. He made a special favourite of Mr Birla, and spent most of his last years as a guest in Birla House.

The Birla family is one of those that, no matter who rules the country, they believe it's really them. And maybe they are right. They have an enormous business empire involved in most areas of industry except perhaps steel. They have factories and warehouses all over India. It has been rumoured that many Congress Party ministers were on their pay-roll, and they were as much in the favour of Mrs Gandhi as they are of Mr Morarji Desai.

When Sanjay wanted closer control of the *Indian Express* since this was the one paper which continued to defy Mrs Gandhi, he insisted that a new board of directors be appointed. Among the names he gave was Mr K. K. Birla, and Mr Birla was also involved in various others of Sanjay's projects. He was one of those who helped Sanjay to further his ambitions, in return for which the Birla empire remained safe. Several times over the years after India became free there were moves to set up inquiries into the Birlas, but none actually materialized. Somehow, at the last minute, it always got cancelled. It is a measure of the influence of the Birlas that, while Mr K. K. Birla has been arrested as part of the Sanjay gang, the new Prime Minister of India, Mr Morarji Desai, still appoints a Birla man as his private secretary where, of course, he has access to all classified papers, past and present.

Why Mr Morarji Desai didn't choose an independent man until at least the various inquiries were over is hard to understand. It looks as though the old connections are still very much alive.

I understand that the present Prime Minister of India is also emulating the Sanjay cult by making sure that his son goes everywhere with him. He makes a great point of always explaining that his son, Mr Kanti Bhai Desai, pays for himself on these trips, but that is not really a good enough explanation. A Prime Minister can have any number of advisers or government officials and cabinet ministers, but he cannot have a member of his family as a right-hand man. His son does not hold any official position in the Government.

It is also rumoured that during the time Mr Desai was Finance Minister, his son used the information close at hand to become a very successful businessman. I firmly believe, and I am sure Mr Desai would agree with me, that for the moment at least India needs leaders who do not compromise at any level whatsoever. The same criticism may be applied to Jag-Jivan Ram, since his son, Mr Shuresh Ram, is also to be seen at public meetings at his father's side, and has been known to carry out negotiations at important levels on behalf of his father.

So what is the new Government of India really like? What are the changes, and what stays the same?

The Janata Party, everyone kept telling me, was born in the jails of India. All opposition parties in India saw their leaders put in jails, and there seemed little hope of their being released until Mrs Gandhi arranged the elections. Jai Prakash Narayan had been saying for some time that India needed a new party to unite the opposition, otherwise the Congress Party would be in power for ever. But no one took any notice. The opposition party leaders had felt that their interest would not best be served by uniting. It was also true that none of them had really believed that Gandhian ways were the only answer. Excepting a few younger men, I don't think they still truly believe it. But, inadvertently, Mrs Gandhi did make them realize that it was either unite and find an alternative, or remain in a police state for ever. Mrs Gandhi taught them the true value of democracy by being a dictator herself.

So the Janata Party was born because it was their one and only chance of winning the elections once they had been announced. But this unity was created to face a common enemy: Mrs Gandhi and her régime. Essentially, the members of the Janata Party, particularly the older ones, remained as divided as they had always been. Their egos got in the way of real unity, as became clearer with the State Assembly Elections. Until then, at least in public, a united front had been presented. Then a kind of free-for-all began.

Mr Charan Singh, the present Home Affairs Minister, because he belongs to the Jaat community from North India, demanded that more Janata Party tickets be given to 'Jaat' candidates. In fact he grew so upset over it that he went away from Delhi and hid in a country retreat until his demands were met. It became the usual grab for power regardless of ability. Janata Party tickets were given to people because they belonged to a certain man's group. Mr Bahuguna, the present Petroleum Minister, wasn't to be outdone and battled on for his group in Uttar Pradesh. The same was true of Mr Jag-Jivan Ram, the present Defence Minister.

When I visited the various provinces, the struggle to retain power became even more apparent. Nandini Satpathy had been given a Janata Party ticket, yet she had been a very close associate of Mrs Gandhi right through the Emergency, and people in fact named her as part of the 'Kitchen Cabinet'. It seemed that anybody able to pull a few strings could suddenly be forgiven the past and made a legitimate member of the Janata Party. It began with Mr Jag-Jivan Ram, an eminent member of Mrs Gandhi's Cabinet until the very last minute, when he resigned from the Congress Party and the Cabinet a fortnight after the elections were announced.

Mr Ram didn't join the Janata Party until well after the elections were over. In fact he did so during the first Janata Party Conference in Delhi. His election result had always been secure since he had the vote of the untouchables, or the 'scheduled caste' as it is now known in India. When he was asked to join the Janata Party I was quite shocked, because not only was this a purely political move, but once again it weakened the opposition. Once again India had a ruling party with its opposition in complete shambles, and everyone of any stature had joined the Janata Party. This has been one of the major problems of the Indian political scene. The Congress Party alone towered above anything else in both the Houses of Parliament, and that made it so secure that it was unhealthy. You would think that by now the lesson has been learnt not to give any party absolute power. But unfortunately it became clearer day by day that past history had taught nothing. The true interests of the country remained remote from at least our older politicians.

I still had hopes that the younger leaders would rise above personal ambition. But during the State Assembly elections, at least, they were able to do nothing. Mr Chandra Shekhar, the President of the Janata Party, seemed ready to give in to all kinds of pressures and to hand out tickets not always on a basis of merit. Mr Jag-Jivan Ram's arrival among the higher ranks of the Janata Party seemed to clear the way for a lot of others. Despite much opposition from the people, the whole thing was allowed to become a rather shameful display of power-seeking. All idealism seemed to be forgotten during those weeks.

The rest of the country's condition wasn't improving either. Prices were continuing to rise despite the Prime Minister's demands that they be kept down. There was a hunger strike outside the Prime Minister's own residence. And the labour situation was worsening. The crime rate, having gone up dramatically, was continuing to rise. The trains had started to run late, and buses were following suit. Chaos seemed to be increasing every-where. People were expecting miracles to happen because Mrs Gandhi and Sanjay were no longer there, but quite the opposite was being allowed to happen.

Even more distressing, many promises made during the election campaign were not being kept. It happens in every country, I know, but India had just supposedly come out of a dark tunnel, and one thought, perhaps naïvely, that considerably more effort would be made to keep the light from disappearing again. George Fernandes had promised a new kind of budget to make it clear that the Government was taking a new definite direction towards the Gandhian philosophy of 'Back to the Villages'; but the new budget turned out to be the same sort we had always had.

At other levels, government was functioning in more or less the same old ways. A majority of the new ministers still sought to do favours for people in their constituencies, and still gave verbal orders to their officers to remove the necessary file, or to do a deal they were concerned with quickly, never mind how long others had been waiting. The officers were still carrying out their orders, because unless they did so they faced transfer or lost promotion.

The only way to solve such problems is to make sure that day-to-day things start to get done without bribes or recommendations being necessary. People go to ministers or officers because that is the only way, and unless this changes, whichever the Government in power, the outcome will be the same.

We need to do something about the small ordinary things in our lives – and the Janata Party has so far been unable to change much. Things like my mother having to spend days to persuade somebody to connect the water supply and put the electricity meter in the house my parents had just bought. In the end they decided to pay the normal bribe for this kind of request and the job got done. It remains true that for routine things like a request for a transfer or an application for a better job, one needs influence, and that this is what complicates life so much.

It can be taken to the extreme where, if a boy or girl fails an exam, it does not occur to the parents that their child may be unable to pass. In the majority of cases, they simply go and bribe the examiner. Sometimes they don't even bother to do that; they just threaten to beat him up. I talked to my old tutor, Mrs Johri, in my former college, and we discussed how the situation was now. She said rather wistfully that life was far from easy. There had been a change of attitude among people.

They no longer sent their children so much to educate themselves as to get a better job or a better husband, as the case might be. She also told me that since the emphasis had shifted from education to achievement, then if the son failed the exam it had little meaning except that people might think he was not very clever. So the easiest way out was to make sure that he passed the exam. I have an aunt who kept doing this with both her sons. The result is that both the children have Bachelor of Arts degrees, but are utterly and completely stupid. In fact, if I told them to hold a ten-minute conversation intelligently about any subject they chose, they would find it impossible.

This curious habit of not curing the illness but of just abolishing the symptoms is very widespread, and as long as it remains there is little anyone can do. One interesting factor, though, was that the fear of punishment by being put in jail made a number of petty criminals follow the right path during the Emergency. Now that there was less fear of being put in jail, the increase in petty crime came in a sudden wave. In the streets of Delhi one kept hearing of gold chains veing snatched from around people's necks, of earrings being pulled off and buses robbed, and so on and so forth. There was also a certain kind of brazen indifference about people. They felt it was unnecessary to apologize if they gave you faulty goods in a shop or wrong change at the bank.

So what has Mrs Gandhi left as her legacy? She has left us with a certain knowledge that the élite of India are complete cowards. They have far too much to lose and no intention of doing so. And if the mass of India hadn't found the weapon of elections in their hands, no solution could have been possible. It was not the educated and the privileged Indian who was responsible for the overthrow of Mrs Gandhi, though in later stages the élite did begin reluctantly to help. It was the masses of India who had nothing to lose and who decided that they would not live in the Kingdom of Evil. I remember driving through a small village outside Delhi. I stopped the car and walked across the field to talk to some workers, and when I asked who they had voted for and why, their unanimous answer was, 'We voted for Janata Party. Not for any political reasons, because frankly we don't understand them, but we did not want to live in the "Kingdom of Ravana".*

Mrs Gandhi had also left us with a system of government which had tasted the blood of corruption. It had learnt that, if managed properly, you could literally get away with murder and certainly with looting the country on a very large scale. The one good thing she did leave us was to teach us the value of democracy.

Although India had an ancient tradition of democracy in its Panchayet system, for the last few hundred years we had known only either a totally feudal society or foreign rule. When India became free and we chose to have democracy, it was approved of by the masses, but they didn't really know what the alternatives could be. Now I think they have seen how painful and frightening the alternative can be, and so I hope they will guard the future with more care. And they will need to guard it, because Mrs Gandhi allowed corruption to seep through every administrative system. There was no sacrosanct ground left.

It was strange how among the Indian newspapers, after the initial shock and protest, nearly all of them began to toe the

*Ravana is an evil figure in the mythological *Ramayana*.

83

line. The *Statesman* and the *Indian Express* groups of papers were about the only ones who stood their ground. Mr V. C. Shukla (the Censor) had had a talk with most journalists, and they had all understood what was expected of them. In fact, it was with considerable pride that Mr Shukla informed Sanjay that every newspaper had come to heel and had agreed to be its own censor.

But Sanjay, of course, decided to be more thorough. So the Act from India's pre-Independence days called the Prevention of Publication of Objectionable Matter Act was revived through an ordinance which enabled the Government to hear, judge and punish the first appeal before the accused could go to the High Court. But the Government didn't feel that this in itself was enough, so it was given the power to demand cash bonds from editors, printers or publishers who were responsible for only what was known as 'prescribed' material. And it took on the power to close down any press suspected of publishing 'prejudicial' material. Then, of course, the Government decided that there were certain journalists who were still not behaving themselves, so all privileges which enabled them to hear Parliamentary sessions or attend special functions were withdrawn. There were about forty such journalists, among them some of the most eminent, including Kuldip Nayar who was briefly jailed. The Press Council of India was dissolved as a result of pressures brought upon its members by Mr K. K. Birla himself.

Other pressures were put on Mr Ram Nath Goenka, who owned the *Indian Express* group. He was threatened that his son and daughter-in-law would be arrested under MISA. When that had no effect, the Government demanded that Mr Goenka sell the *Indian Express* group. He eventually agreed to sell, but only if the price paid was fair and if it was all paid in 'white' money. This created an impossible situation since it made the *Indian Express* group much too expensive. So it was decided that perhaps it would really be a lot cheaper and more convenient if the board of directors was changed. And so Mr K. K. Birla was made chairman of the board by Sanjay, and another friend of his from his school days, called Kamal Nath, was also made a director.

But of course, despite a number of staff changes brought about by the new board, the *Indian Express* remained reasonably straight in reporting news. So Mr V. C. Shukla decided to stop all advertising in these papers, which was a really considerable blow to Mr Goenka, since it meant a loss of 1.5 million rupees every month.

The fight put up by the *Indian Express* was quite exceptional. Most newspapers just bowed down. The *Times of India* became known as the *Times of Indira*. And the *Hindustan Times* group, being Birla-owned, of course remained pretty faithful to Mrs Gandhi as well.

But what I found most distressing during my stay in India was the fact that, barring some fringe newspapers and magazines, no paper was coming out with any real criticism of the new Government. It had been *Imprint* which talked about how Mr Morarji Desai and Mr Jag-Jivan Ram were both allowing their sons to come into the limelight, despite the certain knowledge that a Sanjay cult was something Indians never wanted to see repeated. I do not remember any other papers raising it at all, and it was the same with all other sorts of fiascos. The tone of the Indian national dailies has remained mellow indeed. Can it be that they are afraid of losing their privileges once again? Or have they got into the habit of not saying anything against the Government?

The most likely reason seems to be that corruption has seeped through every layer, every fold of the nation's fabric. The spirit of the witch-hunt that seems to be gathering momentum in India implies that, 'Now Mrs Gandhi and her associates are no longer in power, things will be different' – as though every fault of our personality, every flaw in our thinking, every wrong in our actions, came from Mrs Gandhi and her associates. But nothing could be further from the truth.

It would be so nice to think that all India needs is for J. P. Narayan to live for a few more years and for Mrs Gandhi never to return to power and all the problems will be solved. But is this so?

India's police force has always been a problem. But now that it has tasted unlimited power during the Emergency, the situation has become more grave. In a sense, it is a problem that has existed for a very long time and is common to almost all countries. But in the developing countries, where the poor and the needy really do have nothing, it is so easy for a uniformed man to exert terror. And the irony is that it is in these countries, and in these circumstances, that you need somebody ultra-sensitive and with an absolute awareness of human rights and the needs of society if he is to be a true protector of the law.

A poor man given little authority and very little security is like a cornered rat and will use or misuse his small authority to the best of his ability. The local police forces in the individual states of British India were the most terrifying in their medieval approach to getting confessions out of prisoners. So much was this so that the rajahs of these states would often suggest to the British Government that they should let their political prisoners go into the state jails, since then they would come out either in a coffin or entirely loyal to the British Government. Fortunately for the Freedom Movement, the British Government did not agree. What the rajahs would have done with Gandhi or Nehru had they been given a chance I dread to think.

In some curious way the Indian police have over the years forgotten the real meaning of 'prevention of crime'. We do not have the concept of the policeman on the beat. They either stand in the middle of a traffic island directing traffic or, if you are unfortunate enough to have to visit a police station, you may see them gossiping or lounging about. If you are so unlucky as actually to have a robbery at your home, they will eventually roll up, shout a few abuses at you, leer at your womenfolk and demand a bribe. Then, if you are willing to fill their pockets, they will leave you without devastating the entire house. Don't for a moment believe that just because you have filled their pockets the burglars may be caught. More often than not the burglars are able to pay them far more than ordinary citizens, so the loyalties of the police remain firmly with the burglar.

If you are poor and are arrested for some crime that you may or may not have committed, you are assumed to be guilty until proven innocent. The routine then is to beat a confession out of a man.

Formidable traditions! These are the institutions within the police force which are largely responsible for the horrors of our current history. If a policeman was told from the day he joined that a man was innocent until proven guilty, or that a confession signed under duress is meaningless, or that civility towards fellow human beings is something that is expected of an officer of the police force, the story might be different. If ordinary simple humanity had found a way of filtering through the ranks of our protectors of law and order, then perhaps today we would not find seriously injured people lying in the street of an Indian city waiting for the police to arrive. An ambulance hasn't got the right to take the injured party to hospital, an onlooker hasn't the right to administer first aid in case it involves moving the injured person. Witnesses are scared to come forward because harassment from the police is not only soul-destroying but also time-consuming.

Most people have a set rule that if they see the victim of an accident lying on the road slowly bleeding to death – and many do – they mustn't stop to help. And under no circumstances should they go to the nearest police station to report it, because if they do somebody will almost certainly accuse them of having caused the accident in the first instance and demand a bribe. The only hope for the poor victim is that there is a working telephone near where he has his accident, because only an anonymous telephone call will be the answer. That also can be pretty difficult since we do not have telephone boxes by the roadside and you need to find a trusting and willing fellow citizen with a telephone in his house. In other words, the police force has seen to it that not only are they devoid of common humanity and a sense of decency, but that every living person in India must be devoid of it too.

These, then, are the sort of traditions India has among its police force. Perhaps on the surface they sound very like many another police force in the world, and perhaps they are; but their methods are far more extreme than any I have seen in any other country.

Now Mrs Gandhi took these traditions and added to them, twisted or exaggerated them, to suit herself. She used every branch of our police force to keep law and order, and to generate fear among the masses. These are the various branches of the police force and intelligence services which were used by her:

1. Border Security Force: armed, originally only for the security of India's frontiers.
2. Central Reserve Police: also armed, and used internally only under special circumstances like communal riots, etc.
3. Research and Analysis Wing of the Cabinet Secretariat: originally devised and used only to check cabinet ministers or people in key positions in India's defence system, etc. But, during the Emergency, this changed and became rather like the

KGB. It was rumoured that there were files on everyone in their offices. People really were made afraid by this since the powers given to RAW were unlimited.

4. Central Bureau of Investigation: the usual old channel through which investigations were done. Now this, too, became more powerful.

5. Central Industrial Security Force: kind of industrial watchman, essentially to make sure no sabotage was done to factories, etc.

6. State or District Police: the normal police force that each state has anyway, for control of traffic, law and order, etc.

This was the massive set-up Mrs Gandhi devised and used during the Emergency, and these do not include the army, navy and air force. Now, this machinery had always existed, but what she did was to give these forces powers that could be used against ordinary citizens. Add to this the fact that anyone in India could be arrested under MISA and DIR, and you have some idea of the nightmare which India suffered in the last twenty or so months of Mrs Gandhi's rule.

There was one special talent which Mrs Gandhi had, and this was to move towards absolute power through existing means, and do it so slowly, almost imperceptibly, so that no one suspected anything. As with the Maintenance of Internal Security Act (MISA) which had existed for many years after being introduced to control extreme left-wing subversive activities, blackmarketeering and smuggling. Later during the Emergency, an amendment was introduced into MISA to control the Tamil Nadu situation. The Central Government had to dismiss Mr M. Karunanidhi's Government there for allowing widespread misuse of Emergency powers and spreading corruption. Apparently Mr Karunanidhi had also indulged in 'veiled threats of secession' from time to time. So the use of MISA to control this situation appeared harmless enough.

This takeover had meant large numbers of arrests. It was said that there had been as many as 9,000 to start with, but that later the figure had come down to 2,000.

Yet no one realized what the tightening of MISA would come to mean as time went on. Similarly, DIR, which was essentially used to arrest people who threatened the sovereignty of India, now quietly changed to being used for anything and anybody.

So Mrs Gandhi had these tools which she sharpened to enable her to rule India without fear.

I suppose the only thing to be said in defence of their activities is that the police were used, like everyone else, to further Mrs Gandhi's and Sanjay's interests. But when the upholders of the law became torturers of men and women, they were doing so of their own accord. A sickness inside them was the cause. Sanjay or Mrs Gandhi didn't go from jail to jail to specify the tortures. These were decided upon by the local police inspector.

Let me illustrate this by mentioning few of the favourite methods used by the police to make people talk during the Emergency. A professor was arrested and tortured because the police wanted information about a friend of his. The torture included swallowing the 'Hyderabadi goli' – a steel rod smeared with chilli powder which was pushed into the man's anus. *India Today* (16 May 1977) did a special article about the methods of torturing used by the police force during the Emergency. The article went on to mention iron nails being hammered into the fingernails of victims; the addict technique, which involved shooting heroin into a victim until he was addicted and then withdrawing it; burning cigarette holes round the neck and breasts of a girl and calling it the 'marriage garland'; 'the telephone', which consisted of delivering sharp blows to both ears simultaneously, often causing excruciatingly painful ruptures of the ear-drums; 'the horseman', which involved the stripping of a victim who was then made to straddle a wooden beam for days with hands and feet tied together; 'the aeroplane', in which torture the victim's hands were tied behind his back with a rope, the rope being then taken over a pulley on to the ceiling and the victim pulled up a few feet above the ground so that he dangled in mid air from his wrists behind him. The beating of the soles of the feet was, of course, the commonest torture of all since it leaves no external marks.

Another case of police brutality, mentioned earlier, comes to mind: that of the arrest of Lawrence Fernandes when the police hoped to get through him to his brother George, who had gone into hiding. After they had arrested Lawrence they proceeded to beat him. Today he still walks with a pronounced limp and has to use a heavy walking stick to move around. There are torture scars on his left leg, and his ordeal in prison has left him highly strung and emotional. In an interview given to *India Today*, Lawrence broke down and wept as he tried to recall his nightmare stay in the prison. 'Those bastards, they had the gall to call me a liar. I'd like their mothers and sisters and wives dragged on the roads and raped as they threatened to rape mine. Would they tolerate that? I would like to take a sword and slaughter those that wanted to rape my mother in front of me. How can anyone expect justice from a police force such as this?'

Lawrence Fernandes talked about how his tortures have affected him emotionally, and how the damage will take a long time to heal. He may heal in time, but I wonder if the scars inflicted by thoughtless criminal brutality of this kind can ever heal from the soul of a nation. It is no good blaming Mrs Gandhi or Sanjay Gandhi or Bansi Lal. None of these people or any of the other ministers were present at the time of the torture. The decision lay in the hands of the individual officer and policeman. All those that gave the orders and all those who carried them out are guilty.

We may need to dig perhaps ever deeper into the consciousness of India to find the real reasons. Maybe it is a legacy of the British Raj, since it was then that a uniformed man became someone to be feared. Such fear made it easier for the British to rule the masses. One single British officer could go into the interior of India with maybe a couple of men, and be perfectly safe. Such was the terror essentially of the white skin – but also of the uniform. The uniform was already there, and besides, the police were given such absolute power during the Emergency that it was difficult for a policeman to do anything else but precisely what he fancied – a bit of torture, a bit of bribery, a bit of bullying – because his actions couldn't be questioned so long as he was in uniform.

We need a reorientation, a complete rethinking of the training of our police force. Also, under no circumstances must we allow the culprits to go free. Because if the culprits remain unpunished, they will be the heroes of tomorrow whom our newly trained, starry-eyed police cadets will blindly copy. It is adding another colossal task to the development programme of India, but really we are already thirty years late with this one. We must not allow another Rajan to die on the torture table in any part of India ever again. Moreover, we should never again allow torture tables or torture chambers anywhere in India.

5 The cause

How was it that the people of India allowed such a situation to develop in the first place? Is it a situation, or is it something that is a part of India's personality, a kind of racial characteristic? This is something about which I have thought a great deal, ever since I first became aware of the dichotomy of the Indian people. I must have been seven when, for the first time, I became angry at seeing a greengrocer hit a hungry cow because the cow had stolen the green leaves of some vegetable. I marched up to him as he raised his stick yet again to hit the cow and said, 'It will be kinder, you know, if you killed it. She won't be hungry any more, and if you manage to eat her as well, then some human beings won't be hungry for a while either.' The shopkeeper had looked at me with such pain in his eyes and said, 'Child, you mustn't say things like that. It is sinful even to think about killing a cow.' I had cried then and stamped my feet and said, 'Isn't it a greater sin to torture her with a slow death by starvation?'

That evening a number of our neighbours and the shopkeeper came to my grandfather to moan tearfully about a Brahmin's daughter advocating the killing of a cow. I was given a hiding that day because it wasn't the done thing. From then on I became increasingly aware of this dichotomy among my people. The totally vegetarian, the wholly compassionate Hindu society, where holy men cover their noses not to protect themselves but to protect the insects in the air – where no religious ceremony is ever complete without giving food to the animals, where people will go out looking for an anthill in the midday sun so they can leave some flour beside it, where to turn a beggar away from your door is a sin, and where no matter who comes to your door in need of shelter, drink or food, you must never say no and always offer your best since one never knows 'in what shape or form God will come to your door one day' – this same culture also breeds the people who, with a completely clear conscience, can take their young, widowed daughter or daughter-in-law and abandon her by the banks of the Ganges.

It is firmly believed that once widowed a young girl has no needs or wants, she can easily beg for what little food she may require, and that bathing in the Ganges twice a day will ensure that she is not widowed in her next life. This is not some hair-raising tale of fifty or a hundred years ago; it is still happening today. If you go to the banks of the Ganges, either in Benares or in Haridwar, or a little nearer Delhi, to the banks of the Jumna in Mathura, you will see hundreds of these women clothed in white, with their heads shaven, just sitting beside the river. Some people happily give them food, others see a pretty face and a young body and demand favours in return, which, I might add, are often granted. And quite rightly so, since losing your husband does not automatically switch off all other biological needs. Needless to say, the rate of prostitution, illegitimate births and suicide is very high in these areas.

I was driving through Haryana during my last trip to India. It was late into the night because the car had broken down earlier in the day. We were moving slowly along on the main highway when I began to hear the lowing of a cow as though she was in great pain. There was no village in sight, so I couldn't understand where the cow was. The lowing continued and I began to have visions of the cow being hurt somewhere, so I asked the driver to take a side-turning to investigate. There were about four or five people in the car, so we were not afraid. We didn't have to venture very far before we saw a derelict cottage. The lowing was coming from inside this building.

We went over and found the door of the cottage had a lock on it, but that the cow was definitely inside and banging about as though she was beating herself against the walls. I couldn't bear it, so told the driver and everybody else to just break the door down. Inside there was a thin skeleton of a cow tied to a stake driven into the floor. She had broken both her horns in her attempts to get herself free. I looked at the driver, and he said that this was a custom in Haryana. When a cow became too old to produce milk, then they would take her to a derelict building and tie her up till she died, because if they left her loose she would, of course, make her way back to the house. This way the cow died, but they hadn't really murdered her with their own hands. I told the driver to loose the cow, went outside into the fresh air and was promptly sick.

Isn't it odd how we can neatly pigeonhole our sense of morality? Years ago, when I was little, a neighbour did the very same thing to a little puppy they had acquired and decided they didn't want. They couldn't understand why I wouldn't speak to them after that. So long as the knife that kills the creature is not held in our hands, we are free of the sin. The abandoned creature or human being becomes God's responsibility, so we are free of the sin. I suppose the same kind of terribly personalized, very convenient conscience or sense of morality works all the way down the line. In the most ridiculous and elementary way, it means that an Indian will sweep his house from top to bottom and take the rubbish to dump it just outside his neighbour's front door; or to the bottom of his street from where one of these days a municipal lorry may come and clear it away. It seems all right for him to do that. It also means that so long as you don't urinate on your own back wall, and you choose to use somebody else's, preferably that of a public building, then it's all right to go right ahead.

One step further means that, if you are being dishonest with somebody, then you must make sure that they are not relatives or friends. An example comes to mind. A while back there was the sad case of a little nine-year-old dying of pneumonia in Delhi. The tragedy was that he was in hospital, under medical treatment, and being given antibiotics. The irony was that the antibiotics were manufactured by his grandfather, who never used anything but coloured water in the injection solutions he supplied to chemists and hospitals. The doctors had no way of knowing this, so the child died. When the grandfather was faced with the situation, his answer was not, 'I will not adulterate medicines any more', but 'I had better be careful in future and make two kinds

93

of injections. One for the family and friends and the other for the general public.'

This is, I suppose, best described as a moral blindness, but our problems are many-faceted. The Indian people have suffered from a slowly decaying moral fibre caused first by the repeated Moslem invasions, which began over 800 years ago and ended when the Moguls settled down to rule. And secondly by the English rule which took over the sub-continent and ruled it with a much milder hand.

All these years of foreign rule have meant that loyalty to the Government has become a forgotten concept. In fact, to cheat foreigners successfully has come to be regarded as an act of patriotism. Certain jobs started a tradition of corruption which simply stayed on after Independence. For instance, the Moguls always brought in their own administrators from outside. These administrators left their own country, came to this land of strange customs and found it no trouble at all to charge enormous sums for small favours; after all, they were only here for a very short time and had to make the best of their stay. It was a Mogul custom to bear gifts for those in power. It started with the Emperor and filtered all the way down the line to the lowest of low officials.

Since the Moslem invasions lasted eight hundred years, their customs slowly became incorporated into Hindu culture. One would really need to go back to ancient India to look for the true Hindu traditions. But during the years of the Moslem invasions, the moral backbone of the nation was slowly broken. The Hindu was eventually completely and totally cowed. It took a lot of doing, but it was a systematic destruction. The Moslems first destroyed the Hindu God. Thousands and thousands of Hindu temples were erased from the landscape of India, the ones that remained being converted into mosques. The temple at the birthplace of Rama became a mosque. The temple at the birth-place of Krishna also became a mosque. The temple of Baba Vishwanath in Benares is still a mosque, though the Hindus built another temple beside it eventually. The temple of Somanath not only had its treasure stolen and its gates taken away, but the statue itself to this day forms the steps of the mosque in Ghazni.

The mass of the population of India waited for their God to strike the invader with thunder and lightning. But God, of course, has a habit of turning deaf and blind every now and then, so the sword of Mahmood Ghaznavi shone and thundered again and again across the plains of India. Not content with the destruction of the temples, the invader burnt libraries. Hindu culture has always believed that to burn or destroy or, indeed, even to insult a book by tearing it or stepping on it is a sin. But the invader cared for nothing: scholars were killed, universities destroyed, women raped while the population of India prayed for a miracle. It was, in fact, during these politically dark ages that a new concept of God was born in India. The Hindu God had formerly been a loving, forgiving, benevolent father; now he became vengeful, destructive, unforgiving and a flattery-loving monster. It is during this time that the Hindu women went into purdah, that child marriages began and arranged marriages became established, and a sense of shame at having a daughter at all became the custom.

There were also economic reasons which brought about these changes. A devastated country needs men to take care of what is left. There were battle scars all over north India, and the land needed to be cared for, the cattle to be looked after, and so the change came about. It is still painful to think that it had to come, for this had been the one culture where the universality of the law about men being superior didn't apply. Woman, if anything, was more equal than her man. The Hindu even has an incarnation of God which is half woman, half man. So it is sad that this extraordinary concept changed and became like anywhere else in the world.

A number of lovers of the Mogul arts, music and architecture may be deeply offended by my assessment, but nevertheless it is what happened. People felt it easier to marry off their daughter while still a baby since the responsibility for protecting her honour was then no longer theirs. I remember my grandmother telling me of the days when, from the moment she and her sisters reached puberty, they were not allowed to wear bright colours or to wear perfume or any kind of make-up. When they went out, they had to cover themselves with a plain white sheet so that under no circumstances would they attract the attention of a man. This does not mean that rapes never happened in Hindu India. But the woman has been the most respected member of society in the Hindu culture from time immemorial. She is the creator, the mother; others may come and touch her feet and ask for blessing, but under no circumstances is a woman allowed to touch anyone's feet except her husband's. I remember that I wanted to touch my father's feet to get his blessing, and he laughingly refused to let me do so. Because, of course, being a woman and a potential mother I was the creator and an object of worship.

There was also a very strict code stating that, for a man, the women from your street, or from your village, could only be regarded as your sisters or your mothers. This was taken so far by Hindu religious law that you were never allowed to marry a girl from your village or your clan. These were no doubt some of the reasons why the Hindu went into a kind of daze under the assault of the Moslem invasion. Theirs was a culture where the scholar was never killed, where temples were sacred ground – and not only the temples of the Hindu faith. The Hindu philosophy was never a dogma, and so it never laid down the rules about what or whose is the right road to God. The usual answer given to this question had always been, 'Whatever seems right to you is the one, because, after all, nobody has come back to tell us of the right road yet.' It is not therefore surprising that the invasion of the Moslem soldiers left India in a state of shock which must have been very similar to the state of mind a woman experiences after she has been raped.

The Moslems settled and slowly became a part of the north Indian scene. The Hindu was so cowed by this time that bullying Moslems could ritually *halal* (kill) a cow in the middle of a cross-roads in Delhi and people would shut themselves away in their homes and cover their ears with cotton wool so they wouldn't hear the cow; but nobody had the guts to say, 'This is my country, these are the things I love and respect. If you wish to live here, do so, but obey my rules.'

Then came the very much subtler invasion of the British. It was a lot less bloody. But, in its subtlety, it took away the final remains of the backbone of the Indian people. Two hundred years of British rule succeeded in making the Indian feel inferior to his white ruler – something that the Moslem had not succeeded in doing in eight hundred years. It seems amazing that a comparatively new culture can not only invade one of the most ancient and noblest of the world's cultures, and leave it so thoroughly colonized that it not only feels inferior to its young master, but is grateful to him for choosing to rule her.

The corruption in the administration remained in the British Raj, but it was given a new name. *Dali* was the thing that officers of the British Empire expected from the natives for doing favours as well as for remaining nice and fair. The earlier years, during which the East India Company tried to grab territories by fair means or foul, also left their mark on the personality of the Indian people. The East India Company had its rules, such as if the ruler of an Indian State died without leaving an heir, then the state automatically became the property of the East India Company. This actually happened in the State of Jhansi. The name of Jhansi became immortal because the Rani of Jhansi fought for her right to rule her state. The fight became a part of the first War of Independence in 1857 (which the British call the Indian Mutiny). This particular rule of the East India Company has always fascinated me a little, because it illustrates precisely the kind of arrogance by which the British officers acquired and held the colonies of the Empire.

Once the British Raj had become established, and the Indians had stopped questioning the 'Firangee's' right to rule them, then things did ease a little. All had been taken over, and so long as the natives did not think too much, peace prevailed. During these peaceful years the Raj gave us railways, running water supplies and electricity. I am continually being told by old retired Indian Army colonels about these gifts of the Raj. And I always feel a little ungracious that I am unable to accept them as gifts. Gifts are given without a thought for one's self. But these things were bought into existence in the major cities of India, where, of course, the largest number of British officers lived. The railways joined these major cities to make it easier for the rulers to rule this vast country. Electricity and water were provided in the same major cities to make life more comfortable. So shall we say that the gifts were not really gifts, and that the good which came from them happened incidentally.

One very important thing, however, was carefully planned, and, I think, did untold damage. The system of education was entirely changed, and a new system based on British methods was implanted. This was the greatest blunder of the Raj. They succeeded in alienating India from the Indians. It may have had certain usefulness for the colonials, but the price that free India is still paying for it is too high.

There was one similarity between the British Raj and the Moguls in that the English too did not believe in giving the key positions to the natives. In fact, the Indian very rarely made it beyond the office of head clerk. The Government of India and its officers remained British. In the rare circumstances when they did allow an Indian to join their ranks, then that Indian had to come up through the Indian Civil Service exam and be trained in London for a year. Once the brainwashing was complete, then, and only then, would he be allowed to go back and rule alongside his white colleagues.

This practice occasionally produced very sad incidents. I remember once that my father introduced me to a friend, and that later, when I commented about how English he was, my father told me of an incident in this man's youth. He and my father had been to college together. We had better give him a name for the sake of convenience because he is still very influential; let us call him Mr Gupta. So Mr Gupta competed in ICS and was sent to London and returned a year later a changed man. His father was a very wealthy businessman of north India, and when the son returned the family gave a reception to which the Governor was also invited. A number of Mr Gupta's English colleagues came to the reception, and Mr Gupta's father soon realized that he himself was a complete misfit at the function, so went out into the grounds of the house. A little later in the evening, the old man, who always wore the native costume – the dhoti kurta – was trying to sneak back into the bedroom without the guests noticing. But inevitably one of the guests saw him and asked Mr Gupta who the old man was. Mr Gupta looked at the old man and was so ashamed of acknowledging as his father someone who wore native costume that he answered, without the flicker of an eyelash, 'Oh, that is the old gardener.' Needless to say, my father felt so ashamed that he walked out of the reception.

Now, in the independent India of today, a black Sahib rules India. He is a complete stranger to the villager of India. He speaks a different language, does not understand any of the customs, and because of that the villager does not trust him. These are the sort of chasms that the British Raj succeeded in creating among the

Indian people. A people without a backbone easily become ashamed of their own. And the lack of economic security, and the absolute knowledge that unless they copied their white masters they would get no further than head clerk in an office, did not make it easy for them to be proud of their heritage.

I was fortunate as a child, because I had a scholarly father who was well aware of all the shortcomings in my education. He had guts enough to make sure that when I came back from a history lesson at school which had ridiculed India I would be given another lesson about India's real history. He used to say, 'Don't write it in your exam, but make sure that you remember.' It was he who insisted that I must not think of the Indian Mutiny as anything but the First War of Independence. I am grateful to him for those early years, because he gave me a fierce pride in what is my own.

Not very many were so blessed. The invasions of India had begun with the Greeks, who were perhaps the most gentle of our invaders. And as the Mongols and the Huns continued the tradition of sweeping down and looting, then going back again, by the time the Moslem invaders came, the rot had begun. India had split into tiny states, each with its own ruler, and didn't really exist as a nation. This was the reason why, with each attack, it became steadily easier for any visiting army to win a battle. It occasionally occurred to some of the states to join hands, but such attempts never really succeeded, because they were always half-hearted. There are hundreds of tales of great personal bravery shown by various states, but the needs of the nation were very different. Had the Rajputs really united, or the Rajputs and Marathas united, it would have been impossible for anyone to conquer India. But they always allowed themselves to become so involved with the problem of who would head the united forces that every such attempt eventually led to nothing.

This same problem existed even as late as 1857 when the First War of Independence was fought. The loyalties of the Indian forces were split, the princes themselves each wanted to be given more prominent positions, and some waited to save the money that the British were paying them. It was a total disaster.

But this was not all. One more interesting thing had happened. The middle class of India, which forms the essential strength of any nation, had decided to colour themselves in the garb of whoever ruled. During the Mogul rule, the Hindu middle class produced great scholars of Persian and Arabic. This on its own could only have done good, but what went along with it was that they chose not to learn Sanskrit or Hindi. The Mogul rule had partially forced the situation by making it illegal to teach Hindi and Sanskrit in schools. But had the middle class been willing, they could have continued the teaching of their own language in their homes. Many Indians resisted having to give up what was their own, but, unfortunately, those who were willing to give up those things became the ruling classes.

It was not just the language that the influential middle class gave up. Their customs changed, their food changed, their social behaviour changed. Later, the same sort of thing happened during the British Raj. Nehru used to get quite upset if someone reminded him about the fact that, although he had been brought up in Allahabad, in the heart of north India, Hindi was not his language. It was tragic, because it seemed that Hindu culture really only lived among the poor. And since the poor were seldom literate, their Hindu culture was based on traditions and hearsay rather than knowledge. Slowly the inevitable happened, and every area of Hinduism became influenced by it.

Step by step the religion came to be based largely on superstition, and custom to be based on tradition. Even now, when an average Indian talks about the caste system, he does not really know that originally it was no more than a division of labour. You could become a member of any caste according to your ability. It didn't always have to be by birth. Had it not been so, I do not think we could ever have had the Maurya Empire (321-184 B.C.). Chandra Gupta Maurya was the son of a maidservant. He was chosen by the great scholar Chankya and groomed for kingship. Chandra Gupta Maurya became one of the great Hindu emperors. His India eventually stretched to include Afghanistan.

The average Indian knows little enough of his heritage; the educated Indian even less since the most influential class of India today has been educated in the Western way. His heritage is to him mythology and legends. He reads his ancient books in English translations. I am not saying that there are no exceptions to the rule, my father being one such. But, by and large, we have alienated ourselves from our roots. Ideally, our middle class should have become the scholars of Arabic, Persian and English, but should at the same time have remained equally knowledgeable in Sanskrit or Hindi.

This, of course, brought about pressures on the collective consciousness of the Indian people, and the results are very apparent today. The economic insecurity brought about by invasions and foreign rule bred clannishness, nepotism and corruption. The moral insecurity, now mostly born out of ignorance of our own culture and religion, bred bigotry and a totally inflexible and heartless caste system. It also meant that traditions became synonymous with religion.

So, today, India suffers from all of these pressures from her past, and this is what is continuing to destroy her present, and threaten her future. There is one more factor to be added to the dismal image. We are losing what enabled us to survive the trauma of the last few hundred years – our 'code of behaviour'. During the past thirty years this loss has become steadily more apparent. It is possible that the new pressures brought about by industrialization have added to existing problems. The population rise has not helped, and easier communications have brought home to the average Indian how very little he has compared to the rest of the world. All of this has added to the general frustration and dissatisfaction among the masses of India.

But there is a further aspect which makes it even more worrying and sad. This is the kind of ease with which people are rude, uncaring or dishonest, as though there was no shame in it any more. These negative aspects have now become the expected code of behaviour. There is a saying in Hindi which is used to describe a brazen woman: 'The shame of her eyes has died.' The shame usually dies after a lot of struggle. A fourteen-year-old Lolita can be brazen about sex only because her experience has been extensive. So what makes the people of India so brazen? I remember how in my childhood not only would nobody ever dream of pushing you, but nobody ever ran. The question of your being trampled never arose.

There was always a strong sense of moral involvement, so that your problem never remained your own. If a girl was being harassed, any number of people would immediately come to her aid. If two children were throwing stones at each other, any passer-by would tell them off. If somebody was trying to bully a weaker man, there would always be somebody ready to remonstrate with him. There was also a beautiful courtesy in language that was very like the language spoken in the Court of the Emperor. Some people will no doubt think that I am upset about the death of provincialism in the cities of India, but it isn't as simple as that. Respect for other people's property, a pride in one's own ability, compassion for fellow human beings, respect for their womenfolk and a sense of shame if there is a lack of any of these things is what I mean.

The more I analyse the situation the more I feel that at some time in our recent history we must have broken that essential barrier after which the shame of our eyes just continued to die slowly. The first time a man raises his hand to hit a woman, it upsets him and the woman very deeply. But, as time passes and the incident repeats itself, for him to hit her and for her to be hit by him becomes a norm. In the same way, I think the Indian people too have made the lack of a code of behaviour a part of day-to-day normality.

This loss is greater in every way than that which we suffered through the invasions, though I think that this final act of killing our conscience would never have happened had we not already been fairly demoralized through the past. Once the deed was done, then all other circumstances served to move us further along this path of destruction, as I prefer to call it, or 'survival at any cost' as everyone else knows it.

One more thing we have to keep in mind: this particular phenomenon is not happening in India alone. It is a problem of the modern world. Every country has at some time or other passed through such a period of crisis, and has emerged having made a decision to survive and forget anything else. There are differences in the extent to which a country is prepared to go to survive, but essentially it is only a matter of degree.

I believe that, in India, this killing of the conscience of the nation happened in 1947 when India was partitioned. Until this point the Indian people had only fought and killed their enemies. The Indian did not go out to create an economic empire. He did not even go out to create a religious empire. Until Buddha, India had never sent out any missionaries either. The Hindu does not believe in the concepts of 'non-believer' or 'heathen'. Your beliefs are between you and God, and no one else can decide if they are right or wrong. So only when the enemy came and threatened at India's doorstep did the Hindu fight. If any internal battles took place, they were between enemy states.

In 1947, people killed others not because they were enemies but because they were of a different religion. Neighbours killed neighbours because of this, and friends killed friends. Women were raped, children murdered, neighbours' homes looted, all in the name of religion. A whole generation robbed their neighbours, usurped things left in their care as their desperate neighbours fled to India or Pakistan respectively, and these people only prospered because of it. Families around our house, when they discovered that a Moslem neighbour had flown the country, made tunnels through the walls and took possession of everything left behind. People killed other people who had been friends the day before. A little man who used to sell jelly-babies outside our school suddenly went over to a fruit seller who had had a stall right next to his own for years, and knifed him until the old man was dead. I looked out of our window one afternoon and on the road outside saw nine dead bodies. The stench was unbelievable.

But what was even more horrific was the fact that I had known all these people – slightly maybe, but I knew them. The list included the old man who used to come and do cycle repairs; it included a blind beggar; it included a ten-year-old school friend who came looking for shelter and was killed before we could open the door to her. The grisly list could go on for ever.

They told me that it all happened because a train had arrived that morning from Pakistan which should have been full of returning refugees. All of these people who suddenly turned into murdering lunatics had gone to receive their relatives and had found a train full of dead, mutilated bodies. The driver told how the train had been stopped at the border of what was now Pakistan and how the local villagers had come out and killed every passenger. They had left the driver only so that he could drive his gruesome cargo to Delhi. I suppose it does offer an excuse of a kind, but I can never believe that two evils will ever make one right. The fact remains that, for a period of a few weeks, a large portion of the population of the sub-continent went berserk. In that time of madness, instead of looking after their distressed neighbours' property they usurped it, taking over their houses and everything that was in them. Sometimes the murdered children had called their murderer uncle only yesterday.

Once our own house was surrounded by our Moslem neighbours, who held all kinds of weapons in their hands and shouted slogans as they poured petrol around the walls outside. It was lucky that a truckload of soldiers arrived in the nick of time or I wouldn't be here to tell this story.

In the midst of all this madness my parents remained sane. Not only did they give shelter to all those they could help, but they also refused to let anybody bring anything in unless it had been properly bought and paid for. My mother took this to the extreme where, when a servant brought back a pack of cards from a shop which was being burnt near by, as he thought it would stop him from being sleepy during the night watch, she made him take it back to the shop which was by that time ablaze, because, she said, nothing will be brought into this house with anything but good-will. But my parents were very much the exception.

Why should people like my parents have remained different? I believe it was because the essence of the Hindu culture, without superstition or all the crippling tradition, had been kept alive in our house. Ours is a Brahmin household. My father is a writer in English, Hindi and Urdu. He has always believed that one only feels threatened by outside influences because of ignorance of one's roots. And so he thought that it was essential for the family to learn as much as it could about India, the Hindu culture, our beliefs, our literature. We also learned English and whatever else we wanted to learn. He never stopped any of us from leaving India, because he never thought that any of us would ever really be lost to India.

This gift that my family gave us has been vital to me in my years in England.

It is this which I find missing more and more from families whenever I go back. It is this acquisition of peace with one's own self that the middle class of India lost out on when they copied the foreigner blindly. And this is something which has to come from knowledge and so has always been missing from the masses, because of illiteracy.

If more influential people had been sensitive to the depth of their own culture, then it is possible that the 1947 riots would never have happened. The masses knew no better, but those who should have known better didn't either. It was a case of the blind leading the blind. The man who killed Gandhi was a young man from the middle class of India who killed him because he thought that Gandhi was making too many concessions to the Moslems. Thus ignorance of the essential part of our religion bred bigots. Ideally, Hindu religion should not be capable of breeding bigots because it's not a dogma, it's a philosophy.

The people had become so ignorant of their own culture that, in the name of revenge and hatred, they had become capable of doing unbelievable things to their friends, neighbours and acquaintances. The irony was that they prospered on it. Those who had only one house became the owners of three or four houses, or acquired vast amounts of furniture or clothing, or acquired a shop. It is one thing to be a soldier conquering for king and country; it is quite another to murder a neighbour to get hold of his possessions. So, on the one hand, the moral code was being broken in this way; and, on the other, millions of refugees arrived in each country having lost all worldly possessions and sometimes their relatives as well. The refugees had only one aim: to survive by whatever means possible. They did this admirably – they have survived. But a price had to be paid.

Through this fierce need for survival and a new lust for possessing and thriving on what was not one's own, we killed our shame. We all subconsciously copy our parents. The parents whose children had watched them take over the neighbour's house or possessions would never be able to tell their children the difference between right and wrong because the children had learnt two lessons in their formative years. First, to survive at any cost; and secondly, that to usurp the possessions of a friend or neighbour brings only prosperity. The children of 1947 are by now the parents of today in India.

Here was the beginning of the death of our sense of morality. Once the barriers have been broken between the conscience and evil, there is no longer any lower limit. People stop thinking in terms of right and wrong. The rot will pervade every area of our life. Today our relatively educated Indian does not think that to give water to a thirsty man is a natural thing to do; middle-class mothers no longer tell their children that if you hit that small puppy, in your next life you will be a puppy and he will be a small boy hitting you. Middle-class parents no longer teach their children that they must respect their teachers. In today's India, the one who is respected is the one who has survived well. It is the powerful, the rich and the strong who are the objects of worship. The only meditation that the urban Indian ventures into is meditation to acquire more money. All of this is not only because the Independence of India and her partition was in general bungled by the British Government. We knew, or ought to have known, about the rights and wrongs of our actions. After all, we have had the difference explained to us for far longer than has any other people in the world.

In India there is now more than ever a division among the people. On the one hand, there are those with only the one desire, to survive and prosper. If, to do this, they need to sleep with the boss's daughter or to allow him to sleep with theirs, or to give him some money, or to sell their grandmother in the market place, then this is all right since survival is the main thing in life. On the other hand we have the idealists: those who, like my father, were totally aware of what was happening and who understood the bungling politicians and the ambitious businessmen and officials; and who chose to opt out and retire into the villages to get down to the grass roots and try to teach people how to survive with grace. Unfortunately, these have been few and far between, but fortunately they were always present and ultimately were responsible for the overthrow of Mrs Gandhi.

6 Peaceful transition or revolution?

Six hundred and twenty million people! The majority of them are illiterate and live far into the interior of India, but 620 million decided to show Mrs Gandhi that they had had enough. The results of India's last general election astonished the world and devastated the lives of Mrs Gandhi and her family.

What was even stronger than the results was the fact that Mrs Gandhi had held an honest election. In London, when I first heard that India was going to the polls, my reaction had been that of course she must have made sure that she was going to win. After all, dictators don't leave things to chance, do they? But I was wrong this time; she hadn't made sure that she would win.

When I asked her about it, she said that, 'I was misinformed about the facts. Nobody told me the truth.' I asked people who had provided her intelligence sources, and the answers I got were, 'We had to give her the information she wanted to hear. In the past, if anyone had told her anything unpleasant, they would be transferred or lose their jobs.'

So it seems that she really was unaware of the extent of her unpopularity. Mr Bansi Lal and Sanjay were certainly alive to the danger and were against any elections being held for a long time. But Mrs Gandhi believed the intelligence reports. She believed in the vast political rallies that were organized for her, and since Sanjay and Bansi Lal had seen to the hiring of the crowds together with local ministers, they could hardly tell her these had been faked. They had set their own trap, by alienating her from the masses, feeding her only pleasant news and telling her how popular she and Sanjay were.

She similarly caused her own destruction by growing too remote from the people and trusting no one, not even her own party's faithful workers. Had she allowed herself to hear or see, maybe she would never have announced the election; but then, had she been able to hear and see, she would never have allowed things to get into the state they were in.

She believed that the people still loved her enough to forgive her if she asked them. And, of course, had she come back to power after a legitimate election, her rule really would have been absolute and for life. This thought must itself have been a temptation, and so India went to the polls. And all those millions of people, waiting for just such an opportunity, could hardly believe their luck.

The elections were held with total integrity. It could not have been otherwise. And the people of India showed that, however inarticulate they may be, they would not live in the Kingdom of Evil. This was a phrase that was repeated to me time and again by simple villagers. During my research I talked to people all over North India, and their replies were virtually identical. They said, 'We know nothing about politics, and we know that the Nehru family has done us a lot of good, but Mrs Gandhi created a kingdom of evil and it had to go.' Most of these people had benefited a lot during the past eleven years. In states like Haryana, Bihar, Punjab and Rajasthan, the improvements in road works, irrigation and electricity supplies were phenomenal. But it was also in North India that the vasectomy campaign was at its most aggressively intense. It was in these very provinces that the corruption and terrorization of the people by Mrs Gandhi's caucus reached its peak.

Government officials were also angry with her since they had been used to accomplish Sanjay and Bansi Lal's schemes. They had been forced to produce results from the vasectomy drives, and if they failed had their salaries or increments stopped, their car licences taken away, and so on. Their seniority could also be interfered with. People didn't get promotion because they were of merit or had been in the job for the necessary years, but because they happened to be close to the group around Mrs Gandhi.

All this had angered the government officers to the extent where they felt no more loyalty. And when the elections were announced, many of them, particularly in the provinces, went out to the villages to help campaign against her. The villagers were told quite simply, 'If you don't want us to come and do any more vasectomies, for God's sake don't vote for Mrs Gandhi.'

The villagers had already made up their own minds, but this only made them even more determined.

Mrs Gandhi's faith in her decision to hold elections did not waver until Mr Jag-Jivan Ram resigned from the Government and Congress Party. At this point, I was told, a telephone call was made to the election commissioner to try to cancel the elections, but by then it was too late: the whole machinery had been set in motion, and the constitution does not allow for elections to be stopped at such a late stage.

Later, when it looked as if she would even lose in her own constituency, a telephone call from her residence to the local polling officer forbade him to announce the results. But, by that time, the officer knew for certain that she had lost and so refused to obey. This was told to me by a reliable source close to Mrs Gandhi, and has been confirmed by a number of officials and journalists. Apparently it happened at the famous meeting which took place to organize things and 'defend the P.M.'s residence at all costs'. Those present included Sanjay, R. K. Dhavan, Bansi Lal and D. M. Mehta. There were also a number of senior officials there, and these included the Home Secretary and the Inspector-General of Police. They were told that the defence of the Prime Minister's residence meant that all roads leading to it would have to be barricaded, and that the Border Security Force should be seconded to guard it.

It still puzzles me how a person of Mrs Gandhi's intelligence managed to create such an atmosphere of sycophancy around her, and failed to realize how this would eventually lead to her political demise. A member of the present Government laughingly confirmed how Mrs Gandhi's own intelligence machinery had told her lies about the possible election results, and was able to give us precise figures. On the basis of these deliberate miscalculations she was wrongly advised and told that, no matter what, if she herself went to the Indian people and apologized for her mistakes, they would forgive her. Events, of course, proved how unforgiving the masses can be once they know the true nature of a tyrant. Mrs Gandhi is lucky that this was no storming of the Bastille, but just a peaceful election; and that she can live reasonably happily and safely in quite a smart part of New Delhi, and is, to the best of my knowledge, in no danger to life or limb.

Where does this leave us, however? We have a new Government headed by a group of decrepit politicians, at least half of whom were involved in Mrs Gandhi's Government until they proved uncooperative and were thrown in jail. But against this, we have a new wave of enthusiasm among the people. And, of course, we have Mr Jai Prakash Narayan, his vision and his followers. Does all this make of the Indian situation a revolution, albeit a peaceful one, or is it merely a change of government?

I had already talked to the old hands at the game of Indian politics, and been bitterly disappointed. Either they had seemed vulgar or disorganized, or too disinterested, vain or busy being ambitious. Now, I thought, I should see the younger generation, for the names to reckon with on India's new political scene are probably not the old hands, but such new names as Mr Chandra Shekhar (President of the Janata Party), George Fernandes (Minister of Communications), L. K. Advani (Minister of Information and Broadcasting) and Atal Bihari Vajpai (Minister of External Affairs). It was a difficult time to interview these people as it coincided with the State Legislative Assembly elections and they were deeply involved in campaigns. But I did manage to meet quite a few of them between campaigning.

The immediate thing that struck me was the general ease with which they were willing to answer questions. Nobody said to me, 'Draft the questions in advance and let us see them;' nobody kept me waiting. George Fernandes is perhaps the most remarkable. He was for a long time the labour leader in India, and Mrs Gandhi regarded him as one of the most dangerous people around. My meeting with him created a vivid impression. As I arrived at his office, his PA at once let Mr Fernandes know about my arrival. He picked up the phone and said, 'George, Rani is here.' The shock must have registered on my face – a PA calling a minister by his first name, and this in India too. The usual impression is that a poor PA would touch his minister's feet each time he spoke to him if he possibly could. But George's PA smiled at my amazement and said, 'I have known George a long time, and anyway, he likes people to call him by his first name. The first day he arrived in this office, he called in all his officers and introduced himself by saying, "I am George. What are your names?" '.

I was enchanted. At last here was a human being without a label of any sort. In conversation I found him easy to talk to, with his clear-cut, precise mind. I wanted to know how he was coping with this situation, new for him, of being on the other side of the fence. I pointed out that a lot of people had been hinting that he had been given the job so that he would keep quiet and not make many demands or organize too many strikes.

He laughed and said, 'Actually, this question has been posed to me by several union members as well, and I have always begun by saying to them, "Don't ask me about my attitude from the other side of the fence, tell me about your attitude to me. Until a short time ago I was the leader of a number of unions. Today I am your minister, so tell me how you would tackle the situation? How do you see this democratic government, what is your attitude to this government and do you feel you have a stake in this government?" '

He went on to say, 'I am a trade unionist, but I do not represent only the trade-union interest in this Government. I have a job far bigger than just a trade-union job. I have 650 villages in my constituency, and 350 of them do not have drinking water; 250 of the villages are not accessible even by a difficult road. So, I ask you, whom do I represent, the villagers or the workers or the both of them? I think we need to develop a relationship between the Government and the labouring classes. There are so many problems facing workers today: the disparities in wages and working conditions, and there being no employment at all. How does one reconcile these disparities? I have suggested the convening of a Labour Parliament where such questions could be discussed; where we could present the whole case – the whole national case – and ask the workers to debate and to tell us how they are going to divide the cake available. If they can tell us precisely what they think ought to be done about it and what their priorities are, then maybe we will be able to bridge the gap.'

What George is proposing is a dialogue with the industrial workers so that the Government makes them familiar with the larger problems and allows them to feel a part of the masses of

India. Then they can also take into consideration the problems of the agricultural worker, the landless and the unemployed in the villages. Once that has been achieved, there is a possibility that the workers can devise their own programme of priorities in general development. It would then be difficult for them to go back on what they themselves had advised. It seemed to me to be a very practical plan.

George also confessed that he was a Gandhian at heart. It may seem a shocking confession to come from a committed left-winger, but, George said, 'I think the Gandhian way is inevitable. It's the only system that will help the world. I hadn't been educated in it enough, but the last two years have rectified all that.' Elaborating on this theme, George said, 'It is essential that we go back to begin our calculations in terms of the villages. You will find when the new budget appears that the present Government is taking new directions on the national level as well.* The problems facing us are so enormous that this change has to come. Look at this room – there are two air conditioners, six tube lights and four fans going round, and these are totally irrelevant to the fact that 90 per cent of people in my constituency of Muzzfarpur live below the poverty line. The roads of Delhi are surfaced three times a year, so have no pot-holes, but there are millions of villages with no roads at all. So we have to do something, and you will find that some experimenting at the local levels will begin which will later be translated to the national level.'

I asked him if he agreed that there was a despondent feeling among the people of India that nothing much would change.

He answered, 'I don't think there is a despondency, but I think that every now and then one goes through a trough, particularly after having been high. We are going through a trough now. There have been bottled-up feelings, there have been traumatic experiences, and we are only just able to unburden ourselves. The working-class man couldn't do a damn thing about his feelings for the last three years. Newspapers mention the problem of the rise in street crimes. I believe this is not a law-and-order problem alone. It has been aggravated, perhaps, but it will only become more aggravated if we do nothing about finding employment for our young men. We need political stability, which we will get after the State Assembly results and not before. Until that time we cannot

*Alas, it did not happen. The new budget was a disappointment.

take major steps. We have the big problem also that at all levels the people I see in my office every day were involved in the Emergency in some way or other. Now, we can't sack all these people, but I hope that if we, who are at the top, set a correct example, then the past can slowly be cleaned up.'

I then pointed out to him that among the older members it would be difficult to find the kind of moral cleanliness required for such an undertaking. George agreed, and said, 'You know, crime is not just due to decaying moral fibre. Crime is also due to social conditions, and Indian crime is no different. Ninety per cent of our smugglers have always been Moslems; they still are Moslems. Do you know why? Because Moslems don't get jobs in India easily. At least, that is the case in certain parts of India. Give them jobs and they will not be smugglers. I don't think that I can give you a more glaring example. We really have to tackle our social barriers and our economic conditions at the same time. It's no good saying during a talk on television that we are a sectarian state. We have to learn to live our ideals.'

I came out of the office both pleased and hopeful, yet conscious that I mustn't let myself assume that every young member of the new Government was as straightforward and intelligent as George Fernandes.

I also arranged to meet the new Minister of Information, Mr L. K. Advani. The last Minister of Information had quite a reputation with women, but about Mr Advani I heard only nice things. The interview was at ten o'clock in the morning, so I arrived about five minutes early. On the stroke of ten Mr Advani called me in. Indians in general do not take appointments seriously, and it is unheard of for them to take them seriously if they happen to be ministers. So I entered Mr Advani's office feeling that maybe there really was a breath of fresh air blowing through the corridors of Government. Mr. Advani was precisely as everybody had described him: a charming and highly cultured man. He had no qualms whatsoever about giving me an off-the-cuff interview.

I asked him, 'What makes this Government different from previous Governments? Do you think there will be a fundamental move to solve our problems?'

Mr Advani's answer was so direct and simple, yet it gave me a lot of insight into the man's character. He said, 'For the first time in the history of independent India, the people have become aware that, if they so choose, they could overthrow a government, however powerful it might be. And what's more important is that the Government is also aware that the people can throw it out just like that. This, I think, is the most important factor in our relationship with the people. As long as we are afraid that they can decide to get rid of us, it will help us to remain on the straight and narrow path. This is also the one thing which makes us different. Until now, every government in India has been able to deceive the people or pressurize them or make them afraid. Now the people know their power, and I have no doubt whatsoever that they are perfectly capable of using that power again if necessary.'

I then asked him, 'What improvements do you visualize in your own special fields of the media?'

'One area where we have not allowed our television and radio to function is in constructive criticism of the Government. We have also not allowed journalists to question cabinet ministers about their policies freely. We have never in the past invited opposition leaders to put their viewpoints once the members of the Government have expressed theirs. We hope we will be able to put right all these things immediately. I am, as you know, new to this job, and no doubt I will find several other things that are wrong as I go on, but these are the ones I can see immediately.'

We talked on several other subjects connected with the media and the role of the Board of Censors, and I was glad to find that Mr Advani was neither medieval nor Victorian in his views. He talked with common sense and perception. True to his word, a few days after our talk he allowed some ministers to be interviewed on television and later some members of the opposition party also appeared. So he means it, I thought, and if George Fernandes and all these younger members of the Cabinet mean what they say and are prepared to carry out what they threaten, then maybe it has been a revolution. One doubt plagued me – will they remain honest and strong-willed for the time needed, or will the old experts corrupt their lives also? It was a doubt that only time could dispel. Within the next few days I saw and heard several more of these examples of the new rulers, and a kind of euphoria began to take hold of me. A ray of sunshine had appeared on a horizon which had remained dark for so long.

The Union Health Minister, Mr Raj Narain, who defeated Mrs Gandhi in her constituency, travelled in the same plane as

I from Bombay to Delhi. He sat in the ordinary economy class with other fellow passengers, and if it hadn't been for the bright green scarf tied round his head, no one would have ever known that he was a union minister. The same man also arrived one morning at the All-India Medical Institute and joined the queue at the out-patients. Nobody took any notice of the eccentric old man until the doctor himself happened to see him. The doctor was fully aware of the etiquette required when a minister came to the hospital. So, shaken and white-faced, he rushed to his eccentric patient with the green scarf round his head and apologized profusely, asking him to come away from the queue so that he could be attended to immediately. Mr Raj Narain apparently insisted that he would take his turn, but said that if the doctor insisted on his being given privileges he would certainly be suspended from duty because here in the out-patients everyone was the same.

My taxi driver told me another enchanting story about Mr Charan Singh, the Home Affairs Minister, who apparently one night borrowed a taxi driver's vehicle. He had heard that the Delhi police harassed the taxi drivers late at night and took large amounts of money with threats. So he covered himself with a blanket and drove the taxi to the area of Delhi where these events were most common. Apparently he suspended four different police officers that night, then came back to return the taxi to its owner.

It sounds like a story from the *Arabian Nights:* the Kaliph dressing up at night to go out and catch evil men. For India, such things are milestones, and Mr Charan Singh's scrupulous honesty is a legend.

I was just beginning to grow dewy-eyed with all these tales of idealism when the battle began over the tickets for the State Assembly elections. It was as though it had been specially designed for the purpose of jolting me back to reality. What the change of government in India meant, only time would tell. If the idealism survived and gathered momentum, it could become a revolution, but if ambition alone becomes the driving force of the new leaders, then I am afraid it might in the end all mean nothing at all.

7 Idealists

If one is to believe the myths that the Western world hears about India – a land full of poverty, misery and unemployment and, at the same time, of miracle workers, holy men and idealists – then all I needed to do was to walk out of my hotel, and round the first corner I would have met my first idealist. As it happened, it wasn't all that difficult to find my first idealist who was un-involved in the Government. A face had stayed with me ever since I came to India – a face with kindly eyes that were also full of wisdom, and a face that had the personality of a benign Buddha: that of Mr Radha Krishna, the Secretary of the Mahatma Gandhi Peace Foundation.

I went to see him, and talked to him for a long time about my hopes and fears. Mr Radha Krishna and I became friends, and I began to call him 'Dada', which means elder brother in our language. Dada has been involved in the Gandhian movement virtually all his life. And since the time that J. P. Narayan's movement took its present shape, he has been closely involved with it. I needed to know a lot more about Narayan's concept of Total Revolution. But I also knew that Narayan himself was too ill to give me detailed interviews, and that the most I could hope to get from him would be his blessing. So I asked Dada about how different the Movement for Total Revolution was from its predecessors, and whether he thought it could be successful.

Dada's answer was: 'We have to make it successful. There is no other way. We all talk about the demoralization of our masses and the folly of industrialization. These are not problems only of India, but are present in every society today. I believe that this is very largely due to the fact that man has always believed that revolutions are caused exclusively by the economic restructuring of society. This view must change now, for once the economic restructuring has been completed, it is men who handle it and men who let it down. What we must do is to develop the personality of man at the same time as we restructure our industry and our society. We have to go back to the village, we have to talk in terms of cottage industries, otherwise we can have no kind of decentralization and certainly will never be able to do away with the monopolies of the giant industrialists. J. P. decided that we needed to channel the power of our youth after he witnessed the fall of the Gujarat Government. Until that moment, J. P. was still searching for the right road. But it was then that the concept of Total Revolution was born, and it caught the imagination of the people of Bihar. We need to make our people socially, politically, morally and economically aware and articulate. Do you remember that when you came to see me before, you mentioned that the Emergency would have continued for ever had the people not been given the chance to vote? They are not articulate enough to voice their own frustrations, and the people who were capable of becoming the mouthpieces of those illiterate masses had so much to lose that they were not interested. It is this fact that makes it imperative that we succeed in awakening our people.'

I expressed some doubts about the vast numbers of selfless workers who would be required to form the necessary network if the revolution was to take place on a national scale.

Dada smiled and said, 'We already have a network. You forget that the Gandhian Movement has never died. People may not have known about it or written about it, but it's been there strong and steady for the last thirty years. We have workers in almost every part of India. You ought to try and come to our Conference in three days' time in Bombay. J. P. won't be back from Seattle by then, but you will be able to meet everybody else involved. When J. P. does come back, then, of course, we will arrange meetings between you and him.'

1 accepted immediately. Dada asked if I would like to stay with his family in Bombay, but I declined his offer since I have friends

who would have been very offended and hurt had I stayed anywhere else. So I arranged to meet Dada in Bombay, and left him, feeling delighted. I spent the next two days in Delhi pottering in the shops and saw two absolutely dreadful films. Only the Indians can create the kind of film where tragedy after tragedy squeezes every tear and emotion out of the viewer. These films are so far removed from reality that I am always amazed that anybody goes to see them. I once asked an Indian producer why the Indian films were always so unrealistic. He said, in a rather patronizing tone, 'My dear girl, the poor Indian has so little comfort and such a lot of miseries that he has to have some sort of relief. And we give him that in our fantasy land. We really are much more social therapists than film-makers.'

I never have liked Bombay's climate. It's so sticky, and there is so much salt in the air that it seems to hang over you. One's hair turns limp and feels gritty at the end of each day. Then, if you attempt to wash it, matters don't improve much because the water is so dreadfully hard. But to forget my personal misery at my clinging sari, sticky hands and dank hair, I made my way to the college the Serva Seva Sangha had rented for their conference. In the past when I have attended political conferences I have always been disillusioned. They are usually held in such luxury. Politicians sit and discuss old-age pensions, unemployment and poor standards of living, and in the plush surroundings it somehow all appears unreal: a kind of grotesque show put on because it is expected. Mouths move and words come out, but they have nothing whatsoever to do with reality.

But with the Serva Seva Sangha it was different. Their meetings were often held under the trees, or, if they were held in rooms there were only a few rugs on the floor, perhaps a ceiling fan or two, and that was it. The food was also very simple. The only drink, of course, was water. The simplicity of it, and the earnestness with which the conference had been organized, at once struck me as very refreshing. The six hundred delegates, all of whom were full of benevolence and compassion and profoundly involved in India, were to have a healing effect on me, and I was to discover some astonishing things. It was significant that these harmless social workers had been regarded by Mrs Gandhi as her enemies. The majority of them had spent much time in jail during the Emergency. Their ages ranged between twenty and seventy, and some of them had been doing the work all their lives, some had been third-generation Gandhi followers. They took a bare subsistence wage and their ambition seemed only to make the Indian village self-sufficient.

Their basic objective is to restore faith in the village culture, so that young men will no longer need to leave to seek work in the towns. They have also an extensive programme for reorganizing the education system so that this no longer necessarily produces a white-collar worker who is ashamed of any kind of manual labour. Their programme also places much emphasis on the education of women in line with one of Gandhi's sayings: 'If you educate a man you educate an individual, but if you educate a woman you educate society.'

Talking to these field workers, I found that I was beginning to see the Emergency in a different light. Most of them said, 'You know, we were very lucky that she put us in jail, because had she not jailed members of the opposition and political parties as well as us, perhaps the Janata Party wouldn't have been born. But while in jail, such opposite ideals came together that all one can say is that the Emergency was a blessing in disguise.'

This new acceptance of coming together to work for common aims is the most essential part of the movement. And even if it does not work so well in government circles or in the politician's world, then so long as it continues to work at the grass-roots level, the future still holds hope. I talked to many senior members of Serva Seva Sangha, including Narayan Desai, Kshitish Rai-Chaudhari, Ravindra Bhai and Siddha Raj. I learnt from them what J. P. Narayan's Total Revolution really meant.

Let me describe it by first pointing out the major problems. India is an enormous country in which it is difficult to involve people in government. These people are also inarticulate and often ignorant. So ways must be found of bridging the gap between government and people. We also need to emphasize cottage industries, since this will help the village economy and restore faith in the village culture. All of these things will help to restore the villager's dignity and integrity. We need to introduce a new emphasis in education so that people are no longer ashamed of manual labour. We have to do something about the moral and spiritual fibre of our people. J. P. Narayan also feels quite rightly that the people also need to have some kind of power over the politicians so that they cannot take any undue advantages during their years in office. He has suggested introducing a new whip into the electoral system called 'The Power of Recall'. This would mean that if at any time the electors felt that their representative was not working for their interests in parliament, then they could vote to recall him from office.

Total Revolution sees all these aspects as being of equal importance. So, as J. P. Narayan has made it clear, the 'social, political, economic, moral, educational, cultural and spiritual reforms should be brought about simultaneously. Nationwide people's committees are to be formed. These committees will help the villager with all these reforms, and organize each village to govern itself as far as possible, and at the same time become the mouthpiece of the people and liaise between them and the Government.' And while all this is happening, decentralization of industry must be undertaken by encouraging cottage industry in the villages.

J. P. Narayan has realized that we need the young people and their enthusiasm to make the Total Revolution a reality. So along with the people's committees he is uniting the students and calling this force 'Chatra Sangharsh Vahini'. Literally translated, it means 'a young student revolutionary army'. Chatra Sangharsh Vahini will work alongside the people's committees.

Several other things became clear from the conference. It was obvious that all the delegates had thought deeply about the practical application of the concept of Total Revolution. Throughout the Emergency, these people had formed a network messenger service, criss-crossing India to carry the news. They had also worked out how best to use the available resources. Narayan Desai tells with good humour how, 'Everybody went to jail but me. I stayed in the oasis called Gujarat where people like me could live in safety because the State Government was not of the Congress Party. But you know what happened? I missed out on my writing. I had planned such a lot of books that I was going to write when Mrs Gandhi put me in jail. But she never did. So, I still wrote books, but not the ones I had planned.'

In fact he had taken a very active part in the movement, including much propaganda work explaining to the people precisely what dictatorship meant. While talking to him I also learnt a lot about the Bihar Movement.

In 1974, the whole of Bihar had closed its doors for three days in protest against Mrs Gandhi. Sixty million more people remained indoors, and everything was shut down. There was no transport, no shops; there was nothing. The then Chief Minister of Bihar grew so worried at the staggering success of the movement that he brought in *agents provocateurs* from outside to start a riot in the main shopping centre in the city of Patna. Fortunately people like Narayan Desai were present to quieten the situation. As Narayan Desai said, this was the first time he had been aware of how much more powerful a movement can be once it is allowed to filter right down to the villages. He also dispelled my misgivings about the religious fanatics in the Janata Party. According to him, he came into close contact with them while organizing the Bihar Movement. While working alongside them he had discovered that the fanaticism, which had at one time existed all the way down the line in organizations like RSS and Jana Sangha, now existed only at the lower level.

'The hardship of Emergency, and the exchange of ideas during it, helped to start a process of introspection which will extend to having to think on a national scale, because 50 per cent of the members of the Cabinet today belong to one of these two groups. The leadership in both groups is now really aware of the limitation that their kind of patriotism puts upon them. In other words, if they are to rule a country of many religions, and many more small sects within these main religions, and keep the loyalty of the people, they will have to change and teach themselves that an Indian is not only a Hindu, but can be anybody born and brought up in India and who loves it.'

Narayan Desai, Kshitish Rai-Chaudhari and Siddha Raj all said one thing: that it is time to forget the petty differences and to bend towards one another a little so that all can work for the common good. They also said how important it was that the power of the youth and the power of the people should begin to work for the same cause. In other words, an India split into thousands of tiny groups working only for their own interests is no use to anyone. Something that the Emergency showed beyond doubt was that all are perfectly capable of working together for a common cause, and that they must remain working together.

Mr M. N. Razi from Bihar is another person who stands out in my memories of the conference. He is a very refined, gentle, soft-spoken Moslem from Bihar and was largely responsible for involving the Jamaat-i-Islami in the Bihat Movement. It was the first time since the very early days of the freedom movement of India that the Moslem population of India had joined hands and actively taken part in a national movement. This fact impressed me so much that I resolved to take Mr Razi up on his invitation and to visit Bihar after the conference.

But the overwhelming factor in the conference that touched me was the simple, straightforward faith of everybody concerned. India is a land of faith. Miracles still happen in every village. People still have a simple and personal relationship with God. This shines through everything in our political and social life. Many have in the past criticized Vinoba Bhave's Bhudan Movement. The critics said that no farmer in fact ever gave him good land, and that it was a total fiasco. Well, it may have been a fiasco, but to my knowledge India is the only country in the world where you could walk alongside a holy man and witness him go into a village, ask its farmers for some land for the landless, and get it. The quality of land does matter, but let us not belittle the fact that it was given at all. Farmers, after all, tend to regard their land as their most precious possession, and from time immemorial the giving or taking of land has caused feuds, bloodshed and even wars.

But India is a land of faith, as I said before – here a Gandhi can demand that his people sing Hindu hymns in a mosque and read the Koran in a Hindu temple and get away with it. Here a follower of Gandhi decides that the only way to solve the problem of village unemployment is to redistribute the land, so he goes and asks people, and a movement begins. However stumblingly, however slowly it must have worked, the fact remains that the Bhudan Movement spanned many years. It touched many people and moved many more. There is a very special mentality of the Indian people which made it so — the very same mentality was responsible for the success of J. P. Narayan's movement, and the very same faith which was behind the overthrow of Mrs Gandhi.

At the conference I met two women who were full of such faith. One was Urmila Marathe, and the other was Kusum Nargolkar. Urmila was not yet quite twenty-one, but had been in jail for the whole of the Emergency after being arrested at just nineteen. So far as I know she was guilty of having organized groups of women and educating them, and of organizing groups of youths from the villages in Karnatak and doing the same. Plenty of social work and very little else. Oh yes, she had organized a one-day strike in the university as a protest against the Emergency. For this crime she had to spend nineteen months in jail among common criminals, and nearly died of dysentery while there. I asked her if she ever felt like giving up her work, and getting married to have children. She smiled shyly and said, 'Yes, that is a part of life also, but so much needs to be done and I feel that as long as I have breath in my body, I am going to do all I can. If, while working, the rest also happens, then that's good, but if not, then not.'

The determination and the simplicity of belief could be staggering. Kusum Nargolkar's husband had fasted for twenty-five days just before the Emergency ended. In fact, it was on the twenty-fifth day of his fast that Mrs Gandhi announced the elections. His fast had been started as a protest against the Emergency because Mr Nargolkar believed that some people had to die for India. It was to be a fast unto death unless the Emergency was lifted. I asked Kusum how she had felt about her husband's decision to fast till he died. Her answer was, 'I felt very angry when he first decided it, because I felt that Mrs Gandhi would let him die. But when I discovered that he was adamant, then I decided to back him. In fact I toured all the villages with him in the early days of the fast while he could still move about. And do you know, on the first day of the fast every prisoner in every jail in India fasted with him for a day, and letters and telegrams poured in from all over India. My husband felt that, with all this goodwill, God too would listen and either cause the Emergency to be lifted before anything happened or certainly after it. And just look at what happened: on the twenty-fifth day He made Mrs Gandhi believe that whatever anybody else said she must announce the elections. So God couldn't let a good man's life go waste.'

Supposing, I said, that her husband had died. What would she have done then?

She looked down at her feet, a little embarrassed, and said, 'I had decided to die with him if such an occasion arose.'

'What, and leave the work unfinished?'

'Yes,' she said. 'You see, we have worked together in this

Gandhian movement for thirty years. Without him it wouldn't have made any kind of sense.'

I bent down and tried to touch her feet, but she wouldn't let me.

Two people quietly deciding to die slowly for their beloved country: this is what I mean by the faith of the people of India. It is weapons like these that will create the Total Revolution of J. P. Narayan's work in India. If J. P. lives long enough to structure the people's committees with dedicated people of this kind, then his revolution will come alive. I keep my fingers crossed that J. P.'s vision of an economic restructure based on the village and the development of cottage industries of India will work alongside a political, social, educational and moral development of the personality of the people of India. Maybe then the world will have its answer to both communism and capitalism.

8 The new leaders

I looked out of the window of the plane and saw the parched brown of Bihar stretching in front of me – the Bihar of famine, floods, ancient civilizations and monuments, and now the Bihar of Jai Prakash Narayan. A Bihar of revolution. A Bihar where Jai Prakash had succeeded in channelling the energies and the enthusiasms of youth. It is strange how Bihar has been the area in India where reform movements have always been born. Centuries ago, when the Lord Buddha needed to reform existing Hindu traditions, Bihar became the seat of Buddhist religion. Another reform movement, Jainism, was also born and bred in Bihar. Gandhi likewise found that his movement's stronghold was Bihar. And now Jai Prakash Narayan's Total Revolution has taken shape and I hope will flourish here.

I couldn't wait to get to Patna and see where J. P. Narayan had worked and lived, and the people with whom he was still working. The gentle Mr Razi from the Serva Seva Sangha Conference had arranged to meet me and introduce me to anyone I needed to meet. I needed in particular to meet the young students of Bihar on whom Jai Prakash was relying to provide the fire and push needed for his revolution to get a hold.

It was scorching hot when I landed, and there was no sign of Mr Razi. Remembering my mother's words to be careful about taking a taxi, I hovered around the airport lounge and waited. Twenty minutes passed and I thought I had better make my way to the hotel, whatever my mother's advice. There is only one nice hotel in Patna, so I asked the airlines man to find me a taxi and reached the hotel safely. Later, when I eventually traced Mr Razi, it turned out that the cable I had sent to him two days before had never arrived.

Mr Razi arranged for me to meet some of the young men who had been largely responsible for spreading the news during the Emergency and for distributing leaflets in the streets. I was also to meet those who were organizing the women and the various minority communities.

I very much wanted to see and hear how young men and women of India sounded when they were organized and had an aim, for I have always felt that the youth of India is the saddest aspect of all. Years ago, when I was making a documentary film about teen-agers in Delhi University, I had been somewhat critical of the way they wasted their time. I had felt strongly that the choice of what one does with one's time is entirely in one's own hands. The young men and women of India that I came across then were forever complaining about their teachers or their fees, about some useless cause that they had found to hang on to. It made me feel then that they were so negative and so without hope that it could only do harm to a young country. Now J. P. Narayan had chosen these very same teenagers and young men and women in their early twenties to be his right arm. I wanted to know what they were like, and whether Jai Prakash's faith in them was justified.

Mr Razi showed me round J. P.'s house and arranged for every-body to come the following morning so that we could have a long discussion. Walking around the house was a revelation. I remarked that Mrs Gandhi had once called it a palatial residence. But all I could see were two rooms, a bedroom and a sitting room, which were for J.P.'s personal use; the rest was a couple of small offices and a small public library. There was no trace of anything even remotely palatial: it all seemed ordinary and a little shabby, but much loved.

Mr Razi had invited me to a typical Bihari breakfast the next morning before we went on to the meeting. The breakfast was a great success. Arrays of delicate dishes, deliciously cooked by his sister, awaited me when I arrived. Then we went on to J.P.'s house.

A number of young men were waiting, including Nayar Fatami,

the young man responsible for the Moslem community's involvement in the movement. He was the one who had pointed out that if Moslems had chosen to live in India, then they really must participate in matters that concerned the whole of India. He must have run into a lot of criticism from his own people for this principle, but he succeeded in the end. Mr Razi introduced us. and I was immediately struck by the young man's fiery personality. His large eyes seemed to dominate his face, and there was an air of excitement. I asked what he wanted to do now that the first hurdle had been overcome. His answer was immediate, as though he had thought of nothing else and was dying to get it into the open: 'I wish to fight the election and join the State Assembly.'

'And what will you do when you have done that?'

'I wish to better the circumstances of the Moslems of Bihar so that their lives can be improved.'

I was surprised that he should begin by limiting his horizons in such a way, so I said, 'Don't you think you ought to think in terms of not just the Moslem community but of Bihar as a whole? It seems to me that if any real improvement is to come about in India, we have to stop thinking in terms of communities, castes and classes.'

Nayar blushed and stammered a little and then said, 'I didn't mean that I would limit my activities only to the Moslem community, I just meant that they come first in my mind.'

'But should they? Stop belittling yourself by confining your aims.'

There was a hum of approval from all the lads around me, and suddenly a competition for each to have a say before anybody else began. These young men, full of dreams and enthusiasm, were very exciting to meet. Radha Krishna Ji had said to me laughingly in Delhi, 'If you are not a Marxist at twenty, then there is something wrong with you, but if you are still a Marxist at forty, then there is something doubly wrong with you. So what we must try and do is to use the fire of these young fanatics to our advantage. It will stop us from becoming stale, and it will stop them from becoming middle-aged.'

I remembered the words now and began to understand what he had really meant. Until that moment I had felt that the youth of India was being wasted. When I was a student myself, even then, except for a few chosen ones, the students had remained easy prey to any politician's ambitions. There were always large numbers of them who were really not interested in the academic side of student life. I remembered that someone had said to me, 'Why do you feel surprised at anything the Indian student does or does not do? After all, there are only a few frustrations in life and the Indian student has got them all. He is sexually frustrated because he does not have a girl friend. He is educationally frustrated because the education given to him is totally inadequate and does not make him fit to earn his living. And he is economically frustrated because no matter how many degrees he gets, for the majority there will not be a job waiting. So why shouldn't he go on strikes, burn a few buses or beat up a few teachers?'

I had listened with horror. The speaker was right, and it was all true. If you had what is known as a well-connected family, then you would find a job, however bad your examination results. If not, then the future was utterly bleak. I knew that a lot of older students wrote applications all day long, day after day, and nobody even acknowledged them. India seems to be hell-bent upon creating literacy, but literacy does not mean livelihood.

The students of India have always been in the front line wherever there was a Marxist or a left-wing strike. They haven't always cared whether the things they are protesting about have anything to do with their own needs. It has been as though some sort of political activity helped to pass the time of the day. They were like a mob, for they had no aim and no discipline, but only a lot of pent-up energy. Although I felt sad about their problems, I really could not feel sympathy for them. They had always seemed to go for such silly political slogans, such totally non-productive strikes. And burning buses or blowing up railway lines or damaging roads doesn't ever inspire sympathy.

There was, and is, a lot of crime among the younger generation. This is not the organized crime of gangs and groups as the West knows it, but plain and simple petty thieving. The reasons have, of course, been unemployment and the other frustrations already mentioned. At one time the students of Bengal became so unruly because of their involvement with the extreme Marxist Naxalite organization that the population of Bengal was physically afraid of them.

I know this fear well. About twelve years ago, during a visit to India, I travelled back from Jaipur in Rajasthan to Delhi by train. I had my two younger sisters with me, and my two children. We had reserved a first-class compartment, and all was serene and happy until we reached a small suburb of Delhi. Here the train stopped, and hundreds of students tried to board the train as it was pulling away from the station. This is the usual way that students travel, because if they don't actually go into the station they can get away without buying a ticket. When they get to their destination, they jump off as the train slows down. Anyway, these hundreds of students forced their way into all the compartments in the train except ours.

Since we were only women and a couple of children, we took the precaution of bolting the doors from inside. The windows we had to keep open because of the heat, but they, thank God, had a bar across them. The students yelled that we must let them in. We said the compartment was reserved. I was terrified that they would fall off the steps of the compartment, because at least twenty of them were clinging to the door handles and the rods of the window on either side of the compartment. When they realized that I was determined not to open the door, they began to yell obscenities. The train was by now moving really fast, and with each mile their language became more foul and my fear worse.

In the end I pulled the communication cord. I had heard that the trains always have at least a couple of policemen on board. The guard came rushing to the compartment when the train stopped. I explained the situation to him while the students stood around, jeering and entirely unafraid. The guard became as scared as I was and just said, 'Please, just let the train move. They can't get in, so just shut your ears to the abuse and foul language. Once we get into Delhi main station, I will see what I can do. Out here I am helpless.'

As he walked back sheepishly to the rear of the train, I thought to myself, what kind of future is India going to have if these are our rulers of tomorrow?

We were not able to do anything about the students because by the time we pulled into Delhi Station they were nowhere to be seen. I never again travelled by train in India after this incident.

Students burning buildings or buses because an examination paper had been too tough was quite a common incident a few years back. A student told off for misbehaviour could be another reason not only for a strike but for the poor professor being beaten up. The Principal of Meerut College once said to me, 'I can't tell my students not to do anything because I am afraid of them.'

I understood the frustration of the students, but I did not understand or approve of the means they used to express it. But imagine what it must be like to be a reasonably bright student and to know that there is no prospect of a job because you come from a poor family, while a relatively stupid classmate is assured of walking into a job with a four-figure salary because his father is an influential man. But the solution to the problem is not simply to be destructive. Any country, developing or otherwise, needs the cooperation of its young. After all, they are its present and future, and India is no different, but I had felt until that moment in Bihar that to channel the youth or to use its resources constructively would be an impossible task.

Now, remembering Radha Krishna Ji's words, I realized that the most important thing about the young men and women of India is that they are looking for a purpose. There is a drive, a fire, an enthusiasm in them as there is in young people everywhere else in the world. But, like a double-edged weapon, when it has no direction it destroys or becomes dulled and rusty. On the other hand, it is the fire of these young men which might possibly cleanse our politics of corruption.

It was this that Jai Prakash Narayan had seen happen in the Gujarat students' movement. The sheer force had been terrifying. The young have nothing to lose, so they fight with all that they have got. They hold their lives in the palms of their hands to throw to the lions when necessary. Jai Prakash Narayan is a perceptive man, after all, and he knew that the old hands at the game have the experience that a movement such as his needs to get it off the ground, but not the force which will give it momentum. So if the Total Revolution is to sweep the country and set the hearts of the people alight, the momentum will have to come from these starry-eyed young men and women.

They have a long way to go before a system of education evolves which will take away their frustration and solve the problem of unemployment, but in the meantime India needs them to make Total Revolution a reality. I hoped, as I looked around at their faces, that the newly acquired purpose for living would manage to tame the violence.

The boys round the table included Arvind Kumar, Narendra, A. K. Shahi, Subhmurti, Dinesh and others. We had a long, noisy, table-bashing discussion, and two things became very clear. First, Jai Prakash Narayan is right when he says that hope lies in the power of the young. Secondly, the youth of Jai Prakash is powerful and determined but as yet has no sense of direction. This is a serious matter, for it makes them like a giant who does not know his strength and certainly does not know how to use it.

When I asked them what they thought should be happening, the answers were almost always as though off the tops of their heads. One of them said, 'The biggest problem we have is illiteracy. If we only solve illiteracy it will also solve unemployment.'

I gently pointed out that literacy will only produce even greater numbers of people who are ashamed of doing manual work. Wasn't this one of the major problems facing India now, and did he really think it was fair to increase the problem?

They all sat and thought about it for a bit and said, 'Perhaps we should put literacy coupled with pride in labour as our first priority.'

Again I had to point out that perhaps it would be better if a real emphasis in education relevant to India could be worked out. Once having done that, you could proceed to educate the people.

These boys know the disease, but they do not know how to treat it. Yet they are willing to learn and listen and to work very hard. One of them said, 'If J.P.'s movement hadn't happened when it did, I think I would have killed myself by now. A lot of my friends who couldn't get any jobs after their degrees felt so frustrated and useless. The movement made us feel that there is something that we can work for, and contribute in building the future of our country.'

Stories were told of how the Congress Party of India had organized an anti-fascist conference in Patna, and how the boys got in and distributed leaflets entitled 'Madam Hitler' to the delegates. This had been an anti-fascist meeting, and the boys had succeeded in infiltrating the delegates. They had not only given them leaflets, but had also taken them into quiet corners and lectured them about the evils of dictatorship. This had been achieved despite the fact that security was so strict that police outnumbered delegates by two to one. And each delegate had been searched before being allowed into the hall. They were falling about laughing as they told me this. When I asked how they had managed it, they shrugged their shoulders and said, 'Oh, it was easy.' So far as I could gather, the essential thing was that no one person knew how the whole thing worked. They had created small cells, and each cell simply knew its own job. One group would print the material and deliver it at a prearranged place. What happened to the material after was someone else's job.

I pointed out to the young men that I felt that they hadn't been very clear about how they should set about solving problems today. At this point Sachida Babu, Jai Prakash's personal secretary, intervened and said that perhaps he could be of some help. He began to clarify that 'first and foremost now was the involvement of the village in the general running of the country. For this we need to make the people of the villages aware and articulate. The young people must work towards that end now.'

The young men around the table looked grateful and pleased. One of them said, 'You shouldn't worry so much about the fact that we haven't sorted out aims yet. It's because the aims emerged only slowly. In the beginning, when the movement began, the aims were slightly different because we had hoped that if what we ask for is right and just, then the Central Government with Mrs Gandhi will back us. We had asked for the removal of two things – corruption and unemployment. But Mrs Gandhi refused to help us and called us fascists. And so the aims began slowly to take shape differently. And the removal of Mrs Gandhi's dictatorship also became an aim after she declared the Emergency.'

Among those present in this gathering was Mr A. K. Shahi, who was the first to sound a note of scepticism. He said, 'When first Mrs Gandhi lost the election, we became very hopeful about the future. We had set out to do something, and had achieved it, and so far as we were concerned everyone had fought in a united front, extremist elements and middle of the road workers fighting the common enemy alongside each other. But just recently I have begun to have doubts. Did you know that Sachida Babu applied for a Janata Party ticket for the State Assembly and was turned down? Jai Prakash himself had given his blessing, but Mr Chandra Shekhar turned it down. And do you know who got it?

132

A man who has nine inquiries pending for corruption and the misuse of power.'

Everybody around the table became a little emotional at this point, because many had hoped that election tickets would go to idealists. But power and the need for it can make a man drunk beyond reason. And, in trying to please all of its newly acquired members from various political denominations, the Janata Party had created a fiasco.

Sachida Babu, who had been listening to this outburst from his fellow workers, now felt he must say something. 'You know, I have never had political ambitions, but this time everybody said that just a few people who are honest and hard-working in the State Assembly would make a world of difference. A few honest folk would be able to keep some check upon the rest of them. This was the only reason why I agreed to apply. Otherwise there is no need for a person like me to go into politics. I can probably work better where I am.'

Everybody else around the table immediately began to say, 'And now, of course, the assembly will be filled with virtually the same people who were there before the elections.'

'Oh, if only we get a chance. I don't mind dying for India's future, really I don't.'

'If only Jai Prakash lives long enough to form the people's committees. If only all of this doesn't go to waste.'

I began to sense, alongside the strong desire to work and make themselves a part of the dream for a beautiful future, a strong feeling of frustration. The fear that they might not be allowed to work for their dream made their eyes glisten. But these young, earnest and willing faces were India's future. The question was whether our leaders of today could ever become worthy of our leaders of tomorrow. And will the leaders of tomorrow have the maturity to control their own ambitions and energies? A youth movement made too powerful too soon could be a very dangerous thing.

9 The system

The question of whether we are going to be worthy of our youth, and whether they will be able to rise to the occasion, continued to haunt me. Even more important, I needed to know an answer to one very obvious question: while youth has the force necessary to start a revolution, does it also have the maturity to make a success of it? In other words, how is Jai Prakash Narayan planning to tame his tiger? The old hands at the game always come in for criticism, but dedication and deprivation of all but bare necessities does mellow a personality. These elderly Gandhians are not to be easily dazzled by big promises or kept innocent of the pitfalls. But the same does not apply to the young men.

The one person who could have answered all these questions and set my mind at rest was Jai Prakash Narayan himself. I therefore decided I must see him.

Jai Prakash has been a powerful influence on the Indian political scene for a long time. Before India achieved freedom, he worked closely with Mahatma Gandhi and Jawaharlal Nehru. He was particularly close to Gandhi, and his wife, Prabhavat Devi, was like an adopted daughter of Gandhi. A greatly respected and loved man of much charm and a will of iron – that is Jai Prakash Narayan. In my family, too, J.P. has always been much admired. In fact my father wanted to join his movement in the early 1970s. But he had had a coronary and so we thought it would be difficult for him to take the strain.

Jai Prakash Narayan left the active political scene of Delhi after India became free and Gandhi thought the Congress Party ought to be disbanded. Gandhi believed that, before any of India's problems could be solved, the work would have to be done down in the villages. When Vinoba Bhave announced his decision to begin the Bhudan Movement in accordance with Gandhi's wishes, J.P. decided to join him. He worked closely with Vinoba Bhave for several years, but slowly a realization came to him that the movement was not making good use of the resources it had. The movement did seem to be catching people's imaginations. Many workers within the movement were deeply dissatisfied. It was generally believed that the Bhudan Movement, while inspired by Gandhian philosophy, did not use all the methods that Gandhi advocated for the success of such a movement. During those years J.P. was both constantly evolving as a person and developing his own ideas about what ought successfully to be done in India.

All through these years he had remained totally unafraid to say precisely what he believed. In 1969 he came to the absolute conclusion that the answer to India's problems must lie elsewhere. He declared, 'We will have to go back to Gandhi Ji'. This was also the year when Mrs Gandhi was at the peak of her career. But despite this, J.P. began to warn the country against the growing authoritarianism of Mrs Gandhi and her régime. Right through the early 1970s, he fumbled to find the right vehicle from which to launch his protest, and then, at the end of 1973 and early in 1974, he began to talk about organizing the youths and the students of India to save democracy from gradual annihilation.

In February 1974, Jai Prakash visited Ahmedabad in Gujarat. The Gujarat students persuaded him to accept the responsibility of leading them in their 'Thali Bajao' Movement – a movement which had begun because the students were disgusted with the rampant corruption in the State Government and the rising prices and ever-increasing unemployment. The poverty was so great in Gujarat that there was not enough food to go round, while the hoarders in the favour of various ministers continued to benefit from astronomical black-market prices for grain.

Thali means 'a plate' – the students used to bang on an empty metal plate every evening to express the fact that there was no food. This students' movement remained more or less peaceful, despite adverse propaganda by the Central and State Governments. What was interesting about this phenomenon was how it caught the imagination of the people, and the sheer force behind it became quite terrifying. It was in fact one of the examples which Mrs Gandhi kept giving whenever she talked about student unrest.

For Jai Prakash, however, it was a turning point. He now knew with absolute clarity that the answer lay in channeling the student force. It was as though all of J.P.'s life, through its various ups and downs, was leading towards this one moment when the youth made it possible for Jai Prakash to think in terms of Total Revolution. He had the army which he would need to make his vision a reality.

It was then that a seven-pronged programme was announced. Jai Prakash Narayan believed, I think rightly, that revolutions have failed in the world largely because the world has confused the economic restructuring of a society with revolution. A re-structure is necessary, but it cannot have any meaning if the individual fails to advance with it. In other words, Total Revolution means going back to the grass roots through a decentralization of power at all levels. It means that political, economic, social, legal and all other weapons which the Central Government holds in its clutches should be decentralized. This, in turn, means making the village as nearly self-sufficient as possible, and concentrating on cottage industries. While this decentralization is taking place, a social, political, economic, moral, educational, cultural and spiritual development must also take place in each individual. This, of course, means that the system of education has to be totally reorganized. Jai Prakash Narayan believes that no revolution and no reform movement can possibly work if society is isolated from the individual. The development and restructuring of the two must be simultaneous.

In the West, there have been several people during the past decade or two who have believed that this particular concept is vital not only to India but to the world at large. The late Dr. F. J. Schumacher springs to mind instantly. He, along with others, believed that our disillusioned youth, our dying village culture and our lack of pride in whatever we do are all symptoms of the same disease. It is time to heal and develop the individual as well as society.

With all this in mind I set out to return to Bombay to meet Jai Prakash Narayan. He was now a little better after his operation in Seattle. It was still doubtful, however, whether I would be able to get any lengthy interviews with him, but I had hoped that all the materials I had already read about J.P. and his work would be enough. Radha Krishna Ji himself was going to Bombay, and would arrange my meeting with J.P. Time was running out for me, as well. I had been in India nearly eight weeks, and needed to get back to England and my family. In fact, I could only give myself four days in Bombay, so I had to try and see Jai Prakash each day for as long as was possible.

The first day I arrived, I telephoned Mr Abraham, J.P.'s secretary, and asked if Mr Radha Krishna had made the appointment. He told me that a telex had arrived to that effect, and that I should try and get there any time after about 2 p.m. Mr Abraham sounded a little brisk, but I didn't take too much notice.

I arrived at the Express Towers, and Mr Abraham absolutely refused to let me see Jai Prakash. He kept complaining that, 'Radha Krishna Ji has only sent me a telex, and it just isn't good enough. J.P. is a sick man and nobody seems to give a damn about him.'

I thought that the man was offended because I was sent by Radha Krishna Ji and he had felt slighted. So I tried to pacify him by saying, 'Well, never mind, if it's not possible to see him today I can come tomorrow.'

He said, 'Tomorrow morning is a possibility, but you must telephone me in the morning and I will tell you how he is feeling.'

I agreed, and went off to meet a number of others who had known and worked with Jai Prakash. Some were family members, who had admired him greatly, and others had known him as a public figure. The more I talked the more enthusiastic I felt and the more at peace I became. There was a general air of hope following a miracle. Next day Jai Prakash Narayan had dyalisis and was exhausted and unable to see anyone.

That night Radha Krishna Ji arrived in Bombay and told me that he was meeting J.P. early the next morning. Why didn't I come along? I was overjoyed, of course. Further discussion with Radha Krishna Ji made it clear that it would be virtually impossible actually to interview Jai Prakash as he was too ill for anything except to give his blessing. But Radha Krishna Ji and I talked about the possibilities of a film, not on the life of Jai Prakash Narayan but on the principles he stands for. Radha Krishna Ji seemed keen and thought it was essential for a way to be found to let Jai Prakash's message reach not only every village in India, but all over the world. He suggested that perhaps I should talk to Jai Prakash about it. I agreed and said, 'If I am to get involved in this film, then it must be made for the world market and the proceeds must go back to J.P.'s movement. I would need a letter from Jai Prakash to give me an exclusive from him to make this film.' Radha Krishna Ji said, 'That shouldn't be difficult.'

The next morning I was at Express Towers at 9.30 a.m. precisely. I went up to the guest suite where Jai Prakash was staying. The place was teeming with politicians, relatives and members of several Gandhi-inspired organizations. I saw Mr Abraham, and as he talked to those who were leaders in India, his grin stretched from ear to ear and he bustled about getting them cups of coffee and even managing a biscuit or two. He was ready to do anything for them. Then he saw me, and for some reason decided that I was the least important person there so said to me, 'I am afraid you won't be able to see Jai Prakash. He is not very well and he has to have this old shunt removed from his arm today, so I am very sorry . . .''

Before I could open my mouth, the great benevolent presence of Radha Krishna Ji was before me and I breathed a sigh of relief and knew my troubles were over. He just beamed and said, 'Come and sit down,' and despite protests from Mr Abraham, I saw J.P. that morning for about fifteen minutes. I told him about the film and he was very excited. He thought that it would be one way the message could be conveyed without being open to misinterpretation. He called Mr Abraham into his room and said, 'I know you have a difficult job and tomorrow is a bad day, but you must make sure that Rani has twenty minutes with me whatever time of day you can make it. She's leaving tomorrow and I have to give her a letter.'

Mr Abraham mumbled a few excuses, but couldn't very well refuse, and so took out the diary and told me to come at 5.30 p.m. the following evening. All of this took place in front of Jai

Prakash. Mr Abraham left the room and the tension left my shoulders. I turned and thanked J.P. He smiled, and I thought, his smile has a similar quality to the smile of Gandhi. It is as though he smiles from the soul. He is a remarkably handsome man, with warm intelligent eyes and a gentle manner. He has the face of a visionary, but also a strong chin. There is a will of iron in this man, I thought. He has the courage of his convictions. I came out of Jai Prakash Narayan's room with Radha Krishna Ji feeling relaxed.

The next twelve hours flew by. I was impatient to get back home to my children. I bought their presents and had dinner with friends. We sat up late into the night, talking about the Emergency and the future. There was a rumour in Bombay that Mrs Gandhi had given an interview to *The Economist* in London, and had predicted in it that she would be back in power within two years. Everyone was agog with excitement. Would she be back? How dared she talk like that to the foreign press? What was wrong with our own journalists and newspapers anyway? If she was to make such a statement, it would have been more fitting had she done so to one of our own journalists. After all, what was the point of involving the world in a speculation about our domestic policies?

I pointed out that, first of all, it was entirely her decision, and for that reason it didn't matter whom she chose to tell. Secondly, maybe she was more certain of accurate reporting in the foreign press. The Indian press, after all, does have a reputation for exaggerating things, and sometimes even distorting them. Nevertheless, everyone there reacted as though, by talking to the outside world, Mrs Gandhi had betrayed them personally. It was a little like an incident that happened to me a long time ago when I went to India to do some filming for a play for BBC 2. I was acting in those days, and the actor who played opposite me, though he looked like an Indian, was in fact English, and the crowds watching the shooting had grown angry that I should have chosen to do a film with an Englishman. It was as though, by doing so, I had attacked their manhood.

The discussions about the pros and cons of this move of Mrs Gandhi's seemed endless, and went on until four in the morning. At that point I decided I had had enough and went home to bed. It had been a good but exhausting day.

I arrived to see Jai Prakash Narayan at twenty past five, a little early, but deliberately so. This time I hadn't insisted upon Radha Krishna Ji being there, only because I thought everything had been arranged by J.P. himself. I arrived to see a room full of people. Mr Abraham again came towards me without his smile and said, 'You will have to wait.'

I said, 'It's all right, I am early.'

He went off, and I thought to myself, I must have done something terrible to this man in my last life. I wonder why his smile disappears every time he sees me? Just then the door opened and the Governor of Maharashtra walked in with an entourage of about twenty people. Mr Abraham put on a smile that looked as if it would fall off the edges of his face. He bustled about, and the Governor was instantly shown in. Mr Abraham turned back to me then, and – yes, that's right, no smile – said, 'It's the Governor. I am afraid you will have to wait.' I shrugged my shoulders. It was only just half-past five. I still had a good hour before I needed to go back to pick up my bags.

I was struck, however, by how differently everybody in J.P.'s entourage behaved towards those whom they considered important. The criteria of importance seemed to be not who was important to Jai Prakash or his work, but who was important in the eyes of those who managed his affairs. Because many of these people were indifferent or sometimes downright rude, even to people like Radha Krishna Ji. They somehow managed to ignore the fact that the workers of Serva Seva Sangha are Jai Prakash Narayan's right arm, and an air of trust and warmth is essential between them. It was vital to public morale that a united front be presented by Jai Prakash and his workers. But this was sadly not the case.

I was repeatedly told that the workers didn't give a damn about J.P., that they only cared about their own ambitions and so on. Yet I, as an outsider who knew these workers, also knew the falsehood of such statements. How much more damage could be done by such statements for those who do not know the workers. And, worse still, how much strain can such repeated statements put on the personal relationship between Jai Prakash himself and the Serva Seva Sangha members.

I began to feel alarmed at yet another aspect here, for it was clear that those who vetted J.P.'s visitors could also do him untold harm unless they genuinely possessed intelligence and sensitivity. I pushed this particular doubt far back in my mind for the moment. One of the gentlemen from the Governor's entourage had stayed behind, and was being offered a cup of coffee by a smiling, ultra-polite Mr Abraham. This gentleman, seeing me there, turned and said, 'Would you like a cup of coffee?' and handed me the cup. Mr Abraham then looked vaguely embarrassed and shuffled off to get another.

At ten past six, the Governor's entourage came out of Jai Prakash Narayan's room. I breathed a sigh of relief and got up to go towards the entrance. But Mr Abraham immediately stopped me and said, 'J.P. needs five minutes' rest now, so please sit down for a few more minutes.' I gritted my teeth and sat down. Just then the door opened again, and a tall distinguished-looking old man in saffron robes came in with about ten others. Mr Abraham looked surprised, but greeted him profusely. He forgot all about J.P.'s need for rest after his long interview with the Governor, and showed the man with the saffron robes in forthwith.

It was then that the alarming nature of the situation began to take a grip on me. These people were the same people who had paid court to Gandhi, to Nehru, and then to Mrs Gandhi. In fact, whosoever happened to be the man of the moment has been paid homage by these sort of people in this very way. Today Jai Prakash Narayan is called 'Lok Nayak', which means 'the leader of the people', so here they were like vultures around him. By using J.P.'s name these days you could get a job, raise money or make a public speech. You could choose your own particular brand of ambition, and J.P.'s name would help you on your way.

Everything, they say, has changed in India. It's a new government; its Ministers are from what used to be the opposition parties. In that, I suppose things have changed, but on the other hand nothing has changed really. The use of flattery to get what you want out of life remains. And, to my knowledge, every leader allows himself willingly to fall victim to it. Nehru was very susceptible to flattery, and so, unfortunately, was Mahatma Gandhi. And we all know how Mrs Gandhi was ruled by flattery. The politicians and so-called dignitaries who polished Sanjay Gandhi's shoes and delivered flowers and other goodies to Mrs Gandhi's door, now, with equal ease, brandished the name of Jai Prakash Narayan. In fact they had been out in the State

Elections, getting votes for themselves on a Janata Party ticket and shouting, 'Long live J. P. Narayan.'

The tragedy of it is, of course, that a man as nice and good as Jai Prakash is by nature an innocent. This is why Gandhi used to be taken in, and this is precisely why I am afraid for J.P. There is, of course, also the element of the man's vanity. He is human, after all. For a long time now he has been called 'a fool', 'a senile old man', 'a frustrated politician' by the press. In fact the journalists went so far to please Mrs Gandhi that they actually said that J.P.'s Total Revolution was his last bid for power. In other words, that before J.P. died he wanted to become Prime Minister of India. Jai Prakash, thank God, at least in all of these areas, has proved them wrong. But he is gullible, and he is an innocent. And therein lies the danger. Visionaries are often totally impractical, and so absorbed in their dream and convinced by their own virtues that they find it impossible to sense danger or smell evil.

J.P. has lately been making statements about his own disillusionment with the Janata Party and the Government. Apparently he is waking up to the fact that they will all let him say what he wishes to say, but do nothing about it so long as that is what suits them. But this disillusionment and the dawning of the truth is comparatively recent. And I am uncertain how deep the realization goes, for to my knowledge the people around him remain the same, as does the chaos in the administration of his office.

As I sat that evening in the Express Tower building waiting to see J. P. Narayan, I became certain that he had never been informed that I was waiting outside. I began to think that here was a man confined to his room because of his illness, but that it was this man on whom India's future depended. His vision and ideals must be allowed to live long after his death. His ideals and dreams may be the only hope for India, but are utterly useless for those who surround him. For them, the ministers, governors, businessmen and politicians were the important ones. These were their useful contacts. But it is the masses that Jai Prakash needs. These so-called politicians, leaders and élite will weep perhaps for two days if Jai Prakash dies, and then forget about him. It is India who will weep for ever if his message is stifled now.

I sat there, growing more gloomy with every passing minute, but still I believed that not even Mr Abraham would go against

J.P.'s own instructions. The hands of the clock kept creeping on, and I began to think that I wouldn't have time to see Jai Prakash Narayan unless the man with saffron robes hurried up. At twenty to seven, the second entourage came out of J.P.'s room and a beaming Abraham saw them off. He came to me then and said, 'I am sorry to have to ask you to wait a little more, because J.P. has asked for a drink of orange.' A glass of orange was prepared and taken to him, and Mr Abraham came back out again to tell me that J.P. was now having difficulties in breathing and he had to call the doctor. Mr Abraham telephoned the doctor, then came to me and said, 'I am afraid it is not possible for you to see him. He is just too exhausted.'

I could have throttled the man. Of course J.P. was exhausted. He had had two long meetings, one after the other. I said to Mr Abraham, 'I am sorry J.P. is tired, but I am afraid I have to go now, I am going back to England tonight.' Mr Abraham then began to feel a twinge of guilt, mustered a rather half-hearted smile and said, 'You must think I am unhelpful.'

'You are unhelpful, and have been ever since I met you, but never mind, that is probably your nature,' I said, holding my handbag tightly so I wouldn't hit him over the head with it. I had to bite my lips to stop myself crying.

The gloom had descended at last. The evil that will stop the good from reaching out to the people is the greatest evil of all. This was what I had just witnessed, and I was shaking from the experience. Somehow I felt that this could do far more damage to India than a dozen Mrs Gandhis and Sanjays put together. Not any of J.P.'s idealism had touched those who surrounded him. Jai Prakash knows that it is not he who is important any more. If his life is to have meaning, then this can only be by making his vision a reality that can be achieved. It will not be the politicians or businessmen or officials that he needs for the realization of his dream; he needs the dream to reach out into every level of the people's consciousness so that they can make of it a reality. And this is the only way. I came out of the Express Towers shocked and in a daze. I was unaware that the tears were streaming down my face, because I had just seen what my mother had meant when she had said, 'Always remember, my darling, the darkest patch in the room is the one under the burning candle. That is what you must guard against.'

I took a taxi, went to pick up my bags and started the long drive to Bombay Airport. On one side the city of Bombay glittered with the night lights, and on the other the sea was still and a kind of jade green. It was all very beautiful, but just under the surface there was such ugliness. The taxi driver kept looking in the mirror and saying, 'Don't cry, Mem Sahib, you will be back soon. You will see your parents again.'

I didn't have the heart to tell him that my tears were not because I was leaving my parents behind, but because I had come up close to the evil right under the shade of all that is wholesome and good, and that I was afraid that this land of my forefathers was in danger of once again having her future snatched from her before she had even had time to look at it properly. The evil of our own creation threatened to stand and prevent us from reaching our salvation, as it had done during the past thousand years. Now was no different.

10 The future

A film director friend once said to me after he had come back
from India: 'It is so strange, that country of yours. When I went
there, I felt I knew all the answers. In the first few days I kept
working out how everything can be put right. But, as the days
turned into weeks, I became more and more unsure. And now that
I am back and away from her, I feel that I know none of the
answers. What I do know is that I love India. She is unique and
beautiful, ugly and frightening all at once. And if someone were
to tell me that I won't be able to go back there again I would
be desolate.'

Perceptive man – that is precisely what one feels. The more one
knows India, the more unsure one becomes. But these are
essentially the reactions of those who have the courage to face
themselves. India is not a country for the squeamish. It is really
for those who have known the deeper, darker shadows that lurk
inside their own personality and have accepted them as a part of
their totality.

I love India as if she was an inseparable part of me. I have
criticized her as only those who truly love have a right to. But this
does not mean that I do not acknowledge her achievements, or
that I could ever do without her.

India has stood on her own for thirty years and has survived.
A democracy of sorts has continued to function, maybe not as
well as one would like, but it has carried on. The people of

India have had a fairly efficient judiciary system, except during the twenty months of the Emergency. Law and order too have been maintained without the use of the army or armed police. She has also survived the wars with China and Pakistan, though the economic price she paid would have been high for any country, let alone a developing, newly independent nation.

Let us not forget that when the British left India she had no industry worth the name. India then did no more than produce raw materials which were sold to the world at ridiculous rates, and bought back as finished products made at sky-high prices. She now produces everything – from sewing needles to jet planes. She produces some of the finest cottons and silks in the world. The world of fashion has been overwhelmed by the beauty of Indian materials.

She has her own doctors, scientists, teachers – maybe not quite enough of them, but she is educating them herself. She has hospitals, universities, libraries and atomic power stations. She also has the tenth highest GNP in the world.

The Indian countryside is also changing. I was travelling through Rajasthan last year, while on a location-hunting trip for a film I hoped to make there. We were going to Kotah from Jaipur. I had explained to my director that this was the desert country of India. After a couple of hours on the road he asked, 'Where the hell is this desert of yours?'

I looked around for the first time and realized what he meant. It was all very green and lush as far as the eye could see. I mean really green. If my memory serves me right, it hadn't been like this a few years back.

During the same trip I went into some villages in the area. It was enchanting to find how many of the villages had quite a few tiny but brick-built houses. There were some transistor radios around, and one village even boasted a tea shop. Another had a school, two temples and a rudimentary village hall where meetings could be held. In this particular village, the houses could show not only a couple of beds with rugs and cushions, but even a chair or two.

The whole thing really didn't look much like the desert village I had imagined. I know that other extremes are also present, but, the fact remains, a large number of villages are cleaner than they used to be and have an air of comparative prosperity about them.

There are better roads and public transport, good hotels, reasonable air services and good trains. India can now also boast a telephone system which allows you to dial London direct. All these things have happened in the last thirty years.

The Indian people have also successfully demonstrated to the world that, when things do go wrong in their country, they are perfectly capable of finding a democratic solution. There were no attempts on Mrs Gandhi's life, or indeed on Sanjay's. Mother and son now live in a perfectly ordinary house without police guards. Even on the night of the election results, when Mrs Gandhi herself was frightened that the people might seek revenge, the people remained entirely peaceful. With great dignity, they came to offer her sympathy, but there were no hysterical scenes of any sort.

All these things that are now there, as well as the things that have been in her past, make India a very special country. So what happens to India now? What solution will preserve and encourage all that is good in her, and destroy what is sick and rotten?

One immediate answer, offered many times, is that it would be far easier to destroy all that is there and begin anew. In other words, to follow the path of Marxist revolution. The world has seen how successful this has been in China, and, after all, China is so like India. So why not a Marxist India?

Why not, indeed? On the surface, it sounds like the most logical solution. India is a land of extremes, of the very rich and very poor. It is over-populated, under-employed and under-fed. There is much corruption, and decay. Very often I have thought that, if only one could sort out the decay, one would solve the problems of India. So it is absolutely the right basis on which to create a Marxist revolution, except that I have never believed that Marxism can work in India, or indeed has been as successful in China as everyone assumes. The price that China is paying for her Marxism is much too high and is bound to leave a mark. China must either modify her attack on her traditions and her destruction of her ancient ways or, in years to come, she will alienate her young generation completely. They will be so disorientated that they will grow to hate the mother that so lovingly gave up her soul to preserve their future.

A revolution of any kind must be something that evolves from the roots of a society. A doctrine taken from outside and forcibly imposed can only be like a skin graft that appears to have taken but in the end fails. Whenever a new way of life has suddenly been imposed from the outside, the results have been melancholy. India has had these foreign ways imposed on her over a long period. They have never provided the answer. Otherwise, the British parliamentary system which India chose to adapt to in 1947 could not have been anything but a success. After all, it has functioned for a long time and very successfully in Britain. The British system of education imposed on India likewise hasn't worked. India needed a system of education which taught the average man how to use his hands to earn a living. Instead, today we produce thousands upon thousands of white-collar workers who are ashamed of any kind of manual work, while the unemployment figures keep on getting worse.

Before the British, the Moguls too had imposed their ways on Hindu society and it had not worked. I know that many beautiful buildings were erected, and some lovely gardens laid out, but let us not confuse a few happy incidents with the development of a nation. The only reason why the Hindu survived even to this extent was because of his deep-rooted religious beliefs. Hindu religion is a way of life. It forms our roots, and if you take away the roots you have someone whose identity is forever under threat. The foreign invasions threatened the roots, and we have seen the result. Marxism destroys the roots, and the effect of that destruction on the population of the countries concerned has been visible in the great hysterical purges which follow every Marxist revolution.

Today, by refusing to accept any good in what was old China, modern China is endangering her future. Perhaps we should coin another concept for revolution as something slow and natural, based on the past and the present of a country, which does not destroy thoughtlessly but preserves all that is worth preserving. Maybe we should call it conservation – because then it will be clear that its aim is not to destroy the past, but to conserve what is best and to develop on this basis.

I also believe that the Indian would only accept Marxism if it managed not to deny him his God. India is, after all, one of the very few countries where you can mention God in quite sophisticated company and not be made to feel foolish for doing so. I suppose an Indianized version of communism could become acceptable to the people of India, but it won't be a truly effective solution, and certainly not a lasting one.

Essentially, and however personalized, communism and God don't go hand in hand. So before Marxism became even a temporary solution, there would have to be a lack of belief in God. Furthermore, communism does not by its nature care much about the means used to achieve results. And belief in God automatically makes one concerned about what methods are applied to reach a goal. Then, of course, there is also the fact that communism relies only on changes brought about by the economic restructure of society. And in any country such as India, where the level of literacy is so low, if any kind of system is to be successful, then the individual consciousness must be saved and developed.

India is moreover a sub-continent, not a compact little nation. There are many Indias, and each one of these Indias has a language and a culture of its own. These Indias and their inhabitants rarely manage to unite for any length of time, and this too would create problems for a Marxist solution, which is based on communes. If India had united at any time during the past eight hundred years or so, foreign rule would have been impossible. I have often wondered whether the fact that our religion also emphasizes individuality has anything to do with this. The Indian has always believed that prayer and meditation are between his God and himself alone. It is believed that you come into this world alone, and go from it alone. The relationships formed in this life are considered to be temporary; the only lasting relationship is that between man and his maker. Maybe this is the reason why we have found it so difficult to unite for any length of time.

The other more obvious reason is perhaps simply economic. India has had her problems in the past: invasions, exploitation, internal wars, a rotting feudal system, extreme poverty, disease and not enough food. Today the most important hurdle facing her population is how to survive. And it is obvious that one would always ensure first the survival of one's own immediate family. Ideals which regard the nation, its unity and betterment, come way down the line after the family has been fed and its future made secure.

Now, in today's India, Nehru came face to face with this inability of the Indian masses to think of themselves as Indians first and foremost when the demand for a linguistic division of

India began. The national language of India is Hindi, which is the language of the north. Whatever the anti-Hindi propaganda may have said, Hindi is the spoken language of about 40 per cent of the Indian population, and is understood by about 60 per cent. Therefore it was the logical choice. The rest of the dozens of languages are spoken and understood only by tiny percentages. But the people from other provinces thought that, since this would give the North Indian an edge over any other regions where jobs were concerned, this must be opposed. They were willing to have even English as the national language, but not Hindi. The reasons were again economic, but it brought home the fact that a lot of the Indians do not understand what belonging to a nation means. They think of themselves as South Indians or Bengalis, or Gujaratis, or Maharashtrians before they think of themselves as Indians.

This division within India will similarly make a Marxist solution almost impossible. One of the most important reasons why a parliamentary democracy has managed at least to stagger on, is that the different states of India govern themselves. They have their own civil service, their own state assemblies, their own ministers. They feel that they are represented in the Lower House in Delhi, yet manage to retain their identity. I cannot see how a Marxist system could make itself flexible enough to suit these situations. Then, of course, each of the provinces is fiercely proud of its culture and language, and in the last thirty years people have fasted until death to ensure that this heritage remains as perfectly preserved as possible. This is another kind of sentiment for which Marxism has no time.

In India, except for the foreign rule, we have a tradition of either feudal or democratic rules. The Hindu Emperor always had great numbers of advisers, nominated by the people because of their expert knowledge in a given area. There are also traditions of the Emperor caring a lot about what people were saying. People could always come to the Emperor with a grudge or a complaint, and it would be sorted out. The dynastic rule had retained this emphasis on people and their needs and demands because democracy has ancient roots in India. And the saying *Janata Janardan*, or 'God that is the people', goes back to the times of the *Vedas*. In fact, so far as I can tell, it has always been there. 'The people matter more than anything else' is a principle that one finds in all the ancient books.

The first democracy in India was established 5,000 years ago in Gujarat, when Lord Krishna was elected the President of Dwarika. In those days it was so devised that a village could in its day-to-day life run itself completely independent of the capital. The only time a villager needed to go to town was either to purchase something special, or if a crime was involved where the penalty could have been death. Otherwise, they had their own 'Panchayat', which took care of their interests, gave them advice, sorted out their disputes. The Panchayat consisted of five respected members of the village community who were elected every year. They had to come from the village, and be nominated by the village. This was to guard against an outsider without a knowledge of the village being elected.

The way the communities elected their representatives to be sent to the capital was also simple and straightforward. There used to be what were known as 'Kulpati'. These were elected by various family groups. *Kul* means 'clan'. So each clan or family chose its leader, and he was sent to the capital to guard their interests. He obviously knew the problems that surrounded that particular clan and was able to give advice based on first-hand knowledge. There were no political parties. Politics in the modern sense didn't come into it. A country needed governing, a people needed looking after, so the best way possible was sought. It involved leaving people alone in their day-to-day living, and in larger issues for them to consult their chosen representatives.

It would be a fantasy to think the ancient system could be brought back. The population increase alone would make it impossible. The clans with the same surname are now too large and too scattered to make choosing a 'Kulpati' a practical task. But since the ancient democratic system cannot be brought back, and Marxism offers no real solution, where does that leave us? I think if we try and analyse some of the basic problems which India needs to sort out, then we can maybe begin to see solutions.

Our parliamentary democracy, introduced when India became free thirty years ago, has not worked as successfully as it should have done, despite the existence of a democratic root system in India. The reasons are several.

First of all, there was the dream Nehru had of westernizing India, and this included industrialization. On the surface it looked harmless enough. India was producing nothing but raw materials, so what could have been more constructive than to give her factories? So factories began to spring up everywhere, huge industrial empires began to be created, people's annual wages began to creep up, and India began to make use of her raw materials herself. What went wrong was the fact that this didn't solve the problems of the villages. Mahatma Gandhi used to say that India lives in the villages. He was right, the majority of our people live not in the glittering cities, but in remote, small villages, and the conditions there grew worse. Six months in the year the average villager remains unemployed. He produces two crops, and in between does nothing. This leaves him to exist well below the poverty line. It also means that the young men don't wish to stay in the villages since they have no future there. All they can see is poverty and unemployment around them, and the city from a distance looks glamorous, full of hope, promise and employment. So there was the exodus to the cities of the young men who should have been helping their fathers to improve the land and organizing work during the non-productive months to supplement the family income.

The cities, of course, do not in reality have employment for the millions of young hopefuls who go there. And so the tragedy becomes complete. The cities become full of disillusioned young men who cannot find work and are forced to turn to begging or petty crime. The pavements of Calcutta, Delhi and Bombay are packed with these homeless and jobless youths. And this is where the epidemics spread, and where prostitution thrives and exploitation is at its worst. All this is happening while the villages are robbed of the young men who could so easily be solving the problems which exist there. The city does not want this extra population, and cannot cope with it; the village needs it to survive, and has lost it.

This was the basic fallacy in the plans to industrialize India. It is the village which is dying, and if that dies, so does India. Any kind of development plan for India must take this fully into account. India has to begin from its grass roots. In the meantime, the age-old system of dividing the land equally between all the sons after the father's death means that there are very few really large farms in India. This makes it difficult to use any of the modern methods of farming – tractors, or dairy equipment, or anything which requires large buildings or heavy machinery.

So land reform is imperative, but it will have to be programmed so as not to go completely against the grain of the farmer's nature or traditions.

Unemployment and poverty also breed lack of respect in one's own ability. In the interior of India, where the poverty can be really frightening, this is very apparent. People can be bullied by everyone – by the landlord, the moneylender, the government official; in fact by anyone who appears to possess more than they have. The resulting apathy towards what happens to their lives is the real killer of progress. The village poor tell themselves that God meant all this to happen to them because of sins in their past life. Since all is God's will, why bother to do anything about it? It is as though virtually the whole nation was going through a suicidal depression and was not bothered about anything.

If someone from outside comes into their midst and goads them on, they respond rather half-heartedly, because basically they would like someone else to sort their problems out for them. They have become a nation of beggars. They sit with their bowls in front of them and hope that someone will donate some food or money.

All of this is very often blamed on the Hindu religion. But this is not justifiable. It is purely and simply the fault of what we have become; it is because of this that whatever is the most convenient for us has become our religion. Religion does not teach you not to make the best of your life. Neither does it teach you that, if you live in a rented house, then no matter how dilapidated it becomes you mustn't yourself do anything to improve it. The fact that it's your home, and that if you made it nice you would be the one to enjoy it, means nothing. Most of the poorer Indian villages remain squalid and should be declared uninhabitable, but nobody does anything about it. The reasons are many, and include this strange belief in fate, and a desire to just sit by the roadside and let the world do something if it will. The other reasons are, first a system of education which makes people ashamed of doing any manual labour, and secondly a degenerated form of caste system which causes feuds and communalism and which also makes it impossible for a high-caste Hindu to clean his own toilet or empty his own dustbins.

I remember a very dear doctor friend of ours who came to England for further studies. His family came with him. We were invited to spend a weekend with them. When we got there I was horrified at the state of their toilet and bathroom. So I asked as tactfully as I could why someone didn't use some bleach, for instance. The doctor's wife looked completely horrified and said, 'But I can't, I am a Brahmin. I wish there were some sweepers here, then it would be easy.'

I persuaded them that putting bleach down the loo wasn't really degrading, and that cleaning a bathroom was no problem at all. And besides, it might make the whole thing less of a health hazard for the kids. They were persuaded, thank God. But the strange thing is that these kinds of beliefs are widespread and in my understanding are not even a part of the Hindu religion. No Hindu religious book says you mustn't clean your toilet yourself, or that you mustn't kill a cow, or that you mustn't eat meat. All these taboos began life as social customs to combat some forgotten problem or other, and came to be incorporated in religion.

So much of the misery, poverty and ill health could be taken care of if all these superstitions were got rid of. The other factor which has been our stumbling block is decay. A decaying national moral fibre allows no development to take place. This decay is a kind of all-enveloping evil. When we talk of any kind of system or organization which is not working in India, or of a plan organized by the Government not being as successful as it ought to be, then the cause is decay. It is this which causes corruption at every level in society. It also helps people to remain detached from each other, and only to think in terms of the safety and well-being of their own family. A man will happily take money for digging tube wells in an area, but dig only half a well and pocket the money for the other half. Cases are known of bridges which were planned and financed but never built, examination papers which were auctioned, contracts which were handed over to undeserving people without a thought for the nation's well-being. All of these stem from the same root, 'moral decay'.

With this as a background it is hardly surprising that the average Indian does not become involved in whatever is happening in India. Unless, that is, the situation becomes so extreme, as it did during the last months of Mrs Gandhi's rule, that it begins to interfere with his daily life. The average Indian does not have much faith in officials, and there is no reason why he should. The government official is not someone who speaks his language or follows his customs, or, indeed, who cares about anything all that much, though there are always some exceptions. He also fleeces the villager, or, at least, that is how the villager sees it. So there is no trust between the administrator and the governed.

Neither is this lack of care or involvement limited to the village. The towns also suffer from the same problem. And this is where it ceases being a problem exclusive to India. It is difficult to become involved in something of which one is only a minute part. A silk weaver is involved in his work: from the silk worm to the actual design and the colour of the fabric, everything is his responsibility; the finished product reflects his creative ability. The same cannot be said of a man who works in a factory which makes motor cars or jet planes, because there is no personal involvement, and so no sense of achievement.

This is perhaps also the reason why people today suffer far more from job dissatisfaction. It goes right through all the professions. Today a general practitioner spends far more time filling in forms than in treating his patients. He is also only responsible so long as the patient is not really ill, after which the patient becomes the hospital's responsibility. This sort of situation leads to widespread dissatisfaction everywhere, but in India the problem is even more highlighted since the need to feel a part of the development of India has to be vital for an Indian's life. It is this, coupled with the ability to earn enough money for their families, which will restore personal pride. Once this happens then the 'decay' will also begin to sort itself out.

How can we set about achieving this? There is one simple answer: our system of education must be orientated to India's needs. We need literacy, but along with that we need an awakening. We need the people to question, probe and care. We need to gear education towards the ultimate goal, where man will learn pride in himself and for whatever work he does. Our schools and colleges need to produce capable, self-confident young men who can earn a living by doing anything. We need to make it as much a part of our personality as the air we breathe. We need to believe that a man who works in the fields, or in the gutter, or who drives a bus, is in no way inferior to the one who sits in an office. We need colleges and schools to teach an appropriate technology which will prove useful in a village, rather than to teach only nuclear physics or philosophy or history, to name but a few. We have to make our own foundations rock solid before we can think in terms of westernizing ourselves.

I think that actually the world itself is beginning to realize that a highly developed technology merely separates a population from its roots. It does not solve problems, but more than likely creates some. We need to know ourselves, and take pride in our heritage before we can develop and remain free from complexes. There is now a great movement awakening in Europe, Canada and America which is forcing people to think that going back to the grass roots is the only answer. When it lost its village culture the Western world lost so much that needs to be rectified. We will all have to simplify our lives and become a little old-fashioned, a bit more involved in mankind, because there is much which is good and deserves to be saved.

In India we have to save the democratic system, because it is the only one through which we can get rid of what is unhealthy and still manage to conserve what is good and wholesome. We have to go back to the village. We need to enable the Indian to hold his head high. We need to rethink our system of education and focus it on our people economically, culturally, spiritually and politically. To do this, all these aspects must become a part of our system of education.

There is one more thing Indians need to expel from their personalities, and that is 'worship of the leader'. We have an age-old tradition in it. During the Mogul rule, this particular need eventually created a new caste of Brahmins. They were called 'the Darshani Brahmins'. Their ritual of early-morning prayer and a bath in the River Jumna included a glimpse of the Mogul Emperor. Unless this was accomplished, these Brahmins would not eat. So the Red Fort at Delhi had a special window built where the Emperor would come and stand so that the Brahmins could look at him, pray, and go and break their fast. But a Brahmin, according to our religion, bows to no one except God, because a Brahmin is a scholar. And knowledge bows to no man.

But we seem to need objects of worship. We worship our politicians, our prime ministers, our holy men, in fact anybody who looks like leading us anywhere. This is what created Mrs Gandhi, and this is what could create someone like her again. It is also this which makes me afraid for the present Government.

We are all human beings, and a crowd bowing low is an ego-boosting experience.

So we have to change and improve so much if we are to make the present change of Government into a revolution. But is this a practical proposition? I have to answer that I do not know. The decentralization of industry, if it was done in carefully planned stages, need not mean the destruction of the large industries. Decentralization can, by providing cottage industry to the villages, complement the existing industrial networks and give the villager employment. It can also stop the waste. Two examples come to mind.

First, India has a great shortage of paper, but farmers all over India burn their rice husks, and have done for hundreds of years. Japan produces rice paper, from just such rice husks. There is no reason why the Indian farmer couldn't do the same.

Secondly, India is short of fertilizers, yet all over India, when a cow or a buffalo gets too old to produce milk, the farmer will sell it quietly, because, of course, to kill it is against his religion. So the butcher who buys them drives them into the jungle late at night, kills them and leaves the carcasses to rot. Valuable fertilizer goes to waste because of superstition.

Cottage industry cannot solve a lot of these problems, and the decentralization of government, so that people can feel more involved in running their own areas, is a more difficult task. We need to do it, because it is the only way a country the size of India can be governed successfully. It would also mean that the thousands of man-hours wasted on journeys into towns to attend to government business or to fight legal battles could be saved. The courts cases tend to drag on so long that they can bankrupt a farmer and his family. Yet he really needs no more than a simple, uncomplicated system of legal rights to take care of his daily problems.

But all this means that politicians and government officials will have to lose some of their powers to local men. And it would be difficult for them to give up. It is their dope, their life-blood. The struggle to achieve this would be a long and hard one. But I do believe we need to try and to succeed.

The democratic system has so far always been only partially successful in any country. The reforms in the system are essential. We cannot sit and blame this system for ever; we have to dirty our own hands and clean the muck from all around us. Not even democracy in England is as much of a people's system as it ought to be. Once one goes into the more remote parts of Scotland, Wales or Yorkshire, one can find an apathy similar to that in India. People are not involved, and the same handful of locals have ruled there for years. America also suffers from the same problem. Equality, freedom and so forth can often exist in name only. So we really need to stop pretending that all is well around us, and to rectify the wrongs.

This reason alone makes the success of true democracy in India vital for the world. It is, after all, the largest democracy the world has. If the reforms succeed there, they have a chance of succeeding anywhere.

There is one man in India who has a similar dream of reforms as I have just described them. He is trying to make it into a reality. This man is, of course, Jai Prakash Narayan. The dream he has is his Total Revolution of man and society – or perhaps the total development of man and society would describe it better.

He is using the youth of India to provide the strength and the fire to the movement. He's using the old existing Gandhian organizations to provide him with the experience and the maturity and the mellowing influence which will also be needed. His plan consists of a seven-pronged development programme which includes a social, political, economic, moral, spiritual, educational and cultural awakening of the people. Jai Prakash believes that all these seven aspects of an individual's personality need to develop simultaneously with an economic restructuring based on the decentralization of big industry. In other words, develop the village and the individual at the same time. He also plans to have a nationwide network of people's committees to act as the voice of the people whenever the need arises. It is hoped that these committees will provide liaison between the centre and the interior. Their bodies will be elected locally and will not be on the Government's pay-roll. It is possible that if Jai Prakash's movement actually takes shape and people's committees are formed, and if a kind of educational system is evolved which emphasizes awareness and development of personality and a teaching of simple technology along with literacy, then maybe, in years to come, we will have teachers who will let the light in, politicians who will want to do good, and policemen whose only job is to preserve law and order.

I know that for India there is no other way, except to let a movement, such as Jai Prakash has in mind, succeed. In a way, if India succeeds in restoring her people's pride and manages to give her drifting young a base and a purpose, then she will have done a great service to the world besides solving her own problems. Because these problems are not India's alone.

But still I am afraid. I am afraid that the existing cancer will succeed in destroying the seeds of J.P.'s revolution. I am afraid that too many shortsighted people will think that the success of this revolution would cause them financial loss. I am afraid that ambitious politicians will also feel reluctant to part with a measure of the power they treasure so much. In fact I can see the evidence of this beginning to happen.

Jai Prakash has lost his usefulness for the politician. He was needed during the elections to get the people's vote. Now he is only someone who is in the way. On the surface, at least, the Janata Party has not fulfilled its election promises. But if Jai Prakash's movement succeeds, then the politicians will face the biggest threat they have ever known. Jai Prakash wishes to incorporate 'the power of recall' in our constitution. This would mean that if a politician at any time ceased to act as a true representative of the interests of the people who elected him, then they would have the power to recall him and elect someone else in his place. Now what right-minded politician would place such a weapon in the hands of the people?

Hence the sceptic in me says that India will stagger on in the way she has done for the past thirty years. There seems very little chance that the Indians will suddenly stop worshipping their leaders. And as long as they continue to do so the danger will still exist of creating another Sanjay and Mrs Gandhi. They would have different names, of course, and be different people, but the essence would be the same. It was not Mrs Gandhi and Sanjay and the caucus who damaged India – it was Indians who damaged India by creating the caucus. It is high time that this realization came home to us. It is time also that we realized that unless we put every ounce of our strength into the dream of Total Revolution, there is no way forward.

Let us for once try not to be practical, intellectually clever and believing only in the tangible truth. Let us be really impractical, unfashionable and naïve, and reach for the stars. Let us back the Total Revolution, however unreal, however impractical it sounds, but let us put all our heart and soul into making a success of it. Perhaps if we really try to make this dream a reality, then the force required to make it possible will give us the momentum which will turn us away from the slippery downhill path leading us to destruction, and place us on the path of a conserver society. If we succeed in turning away from the mouth of the hellhole, then maybe it will still not be too late. And our children and their children will inherit from us a road that will lead them to greener and cleaner pastures.